LIFE IN ANCIENT INDIA
IN
THE AGE OF MANTRAS

LIFE IN ANCIENT INDIA IN THE AGE OF MANTRAS

P. T. SRINIVAS IYENGAR

GYAN

Published by

GYAN

Gyan Publishing House
5, Ansari Road
Daryaganj, New Delhi-110002
Phone: 011-47034999, 9811692060
E-mail: books@gyanbooks.com

Distribution Network
gyanbooks.com
India, USA, Canada, UK, Australia, France

ISBN : 978-81-212-3715-4 (PB)

2nd Impression 2020

Printed at: Gyan Press, Delhi.

LIfe in Ancient India In the Age of Mantras
Author: P. T. Srinivas Iyengar

PREFACE.

THIS is the first of a series of monographs on the History of the Indian people, in which an attempt will be made to reconstruct the life of the people of India, age by age from Indian literature, epigraphical records, and records of foreign travellers. This is a work that can best be done by Indian writers trained in methods of critical investigation; foreign scholars can scarcely do it well, for they have not that intimate knowledge of Indian life as it is to-day, especially in villages which are remote from the railway and the telegraph and the influence of European commerce and where are still preserved most of the customs described in the following pages; and without such knowledge, work of this kind cannot be well done. Nor is it work to be undertaken by scholars of the type of the Pandit, who, however estimable his personal character and ideals in life, sees the past through the mist of tradition and believes that Ancient India was in a golden age when the gods roamed the land and supermen taught the people and who is so devoid of the historical sense that he holds everything he has learnt from tradition must be believed in and that an attempt at verification is sacrilege.

The following is a tentative list of the 'source-books' that have to be used in the investigation :—

The Mantras.
The Brāhmaṇams.
The Sūtras.
The Mahābhāratam and the Rāmāyaṇam.
Buddhist Pali Literature.
Greek Accounts of India.
Asoka's Inscriptions.
Māhabhāshya.

Artha S'āstra and Chānukya Nīti.
Charaka and other Medical Works.
Kāma Sāstra and Nāṭya S'āstra.
Dhanur Veda and Gandharva Veda, S'ilpa S'āstra, [etc.
Roman Accounts of India.
The Andhra and Gupta Inscriptions.
The Purānas.
Buddhist Sanskrit Literature.
Jaina Sanskrit and Prākrit Literature.
The Early Nāṭakas from Bhāsa to Kālidāsa.
The Early Sanskrit Lyrics.
Kathāsaritsāgara.
The Early Tamil Literature.
The Smritis.
Alaṅkāra S'astra.
Astrological Works.
Nīti S'astras.
Panchatantra, (Hindu and Jaina) and other Fables.
The Accounts of the Chinese Travellers.
Harshacharita and other Prose Kāvyas.
The Later Nāṭakas, Kāvyas and Lyrics.
The Tantras.
South Indian Inscriptions.
The Tamil Vaishṇava and S'aiva Prabhandas.
Mīmāmsā Vārtikas, Sāṅkhya Tales, etc.
Chālukya Inscriptions.
Carnatic Inscriptions.

At this point Ancient India ended and Mediæval India began and it closed in the middle of the XIX Century when the Railway and the Telegraph were introduced and the Indian Universities were opened.

Alberuni's Tārikhu-l-Hind.
Rājataraṅgiṇī and Vikramāṅkadeva Charitram.
The Later Tamil Literature.
Prithvi Rāj Rāso and other Hindi bardic Chronicles.
Mitākshara and Aparārka.

Rās Māla and Annals of Rajasthan.
Medātithi, Asahāya and Hemādri.
The Earlier Muhammadan Histories
The Pāṇdya Inscriptions.
Early Bengali, Mahārāshṭri and Hindi Literature.
Mādhava's Smriti Works.
Vijayanagar Inscriptions and Telugu and Canarese Literature.
The Lives of S'aṇkara, Rāmānuja, Madhva and Vallabha.
Later Muhammadan Historians.
Memoirs of Moghul Emperors.
The Accounts of the Earlier European Travellers: Nuñez, Bernier, Tavernier, Manucci, etc.
Modern Smriti Works.
Records of E. I. Companies.
Recent Accounts of Recent India.

This ambitious programme is obviously impossible for a single man to undertake; it requires a syndicate of scholars to work at and is printed here in the hope that its publication will induce competent workers to collaborate with me in the work.

This, the first volume of the series, deals with the age of the Mantras. As a result of the philological, ethnological, geographical, archæological and historical researches of recent years, the boundaries of this age can be fairly accurately fixed to be the XVII and X Centuries B.C. The bulk of the Mantras were probably composed in the middle of this age, about 1500 B.C. This age of the Mantras is treated in this book as one age with definite characteristics that can be described. The age is short enough to be one definite period in the life of the peoples of India referred to in the Mantras, especially considering how slowly manners and customs change in India. European scholars of the earlier days regarded the Rig Veda Mantras as representing a very early age, the Atharva Veda Mantras, a later one and the Yajur Veda Mantras, a still later one. Prof. Bloomfield has proved that parts of the Atharva Veda are as old as the earliest parts of the Rig Veda. "There is no proof that even the oldest parts of the R. V., or the most ancient Hindu tradition accessible historically, exclude the existence of the class of writings entitled to any of the names given to the Atharvan charms; there is no evidence that these writings ever differed in form (metre) or style from those in the existing Atharvan redactions; and finally, there is no positive evidence—barring the *argumentum ex silentio*—that the names current in other texts as designations of Atharvan hymns (bheshajāni, atharvāṇah, aṅgirasah, etc.) were unknown at the earliest period of literary activity" (S. T. B. E., Vol. XLII, p. xxx). But as regards the Yajur Veda, Prof. Macdonnell has recently remarked, that it "introduces us to an epoch of religious and social life, different from that of the Rig Veda. What gives the Yajur Veda the stamp of a new epoch is the position occupied by the sacrifice. In the Rig Veda the sacrifice was merely a means of influencing the will of the gods in favour of the offerer; in the Yajur Veda it has not only become the centre of thought and desire, but its power is now so great that it compels the gods to do the will of the priest" (*Imp. Gaz. Ind.* II, 228). It is strange that a scholar of Prof. Macdonnell's eminence here confounds two quite different things—the object of the Rishis in *composing* the Mantras and the objects of the priests (the adhvaryus, in this case), in *arranging* existing Mantras for ceremonial purposes. The Mantras of the Yajur Veda are half Rik and half prose formula, called Yajus. The Riks of the Rig Veda and the Riks of the Yajur Veda both belong to the same age. Of the prose formulas some are from a remote antiquity, *e.g.*, Vaushaṭ, S'raushaṭ, etc., and others later, but certainly not later than the age of the Mantras. The Mantras were all *composed* for use in sacrifices When at the end of the age of the Mantras, the sacrificial system has become very complicated, it became necessary to compile the Mantras into collections or Samhitās. This compilation was made in the age of the Brahmaṇams. The work of the Adhvaryu being the most difficult, the Adhvaryu-Veda (Yajur Veda) was so compiled that the order of the Mantras was that of a prearranged scheme of sacrifices. According to Indian tradition the Yajur Veda was the first Samhitā, the first compilation of Mantras for a definite purpose; the next probably was the Sāma Veda Samhitā. The Rig and Atharva Veda Samhitās were compiled more to preserve the ancient Mantras from being forgotten than in accordance with any definite ceremonial scheme. Thus though the compilation into Samhitās was done at various times, the Mantras themselves were composed in one age. Indeed Prof. Macdonnell himself admits that "the language of the sacrificial formulas of the Yajur Veda, ... on the whole agrees with that of the Rig Veda. The mythology is still much the same" (*Ib.*); this is because they belong to the same age and both contain selections from the same original material. It is quite true that among the Mantras some are older and others later. Possibly the distance of time that separates the earliest Mantra from the latest one may amount to seven centuries; but undoubtedly the bulk of the Vedic Mantras belong to one definite period of Indian history.

This account of the life of the Indians of the

North-West in the remote age of the early Rishis shows that the people were neither primitive, pastoral tribes devoid of agriculture, commerce and industries as some people have described them; nor were they of a superhuman race living in a golden age of peace and virtue. On the contrary the Rishis were very human men, full of the joy of life and without that pessimistic contempt for the good things of the world which later Rishis, those of the Upanishads, those of the Dars'anas and later teachers of unorthodox systems, like Mahāvīra and Gautama Buddha and modern Āchāryas have filled Indian thought with. The Purāṇas are as responsible for the absurd megalomania in chronological, historical and geographical notions of the Hindus of to-day as the Āchāryas of the last millennium for the hankering for escape from the life of the world which colours all aspirations of Hindus and renders them nerveless in the struggle for life among the nations of the world. If this little book will help to make a few Hindus rise above the limitations of tradition and take a sane view of the past, it will have achieved a useful purpose.

In the following pages, every statement is substantiated by quotations from the Mantras; and as far as possible, the excellent translations of Griffith, Whitney, Muir, and Bloomfield have been quoted. In a very few passages I have made my own translation. In the case of most technical terms of the Vedic Age, I have given the Sanskrit words in brackets; for many of these words have either dropped out, or acquired other meanings in later Sanskrit and this prominent mention of them may prove of interest to Indian readers.

P. T. SRINIVAS IYENGAR.

CONTENTS.

Life in Ancient India.

THE AGE OF THE MANTRAS.

THE earliest sources of information we have about the history of the people of India are the Vedas. The Vedas are four, the Rig Veda, the Yajur Veda, the Sāma Veda and the Atharva Veda. Each Veda is divided into two divisions, an earlier part, called Mantra and a later part, called Brāhmaṇam. The Mantras exist in two forms: (1) a collection in a fixed order, called Samhitā; and (2) stray Mantras, called Khila. The Samhitās exist in various rescensions, differing very little from each other, but to each Samhitā is attached a Brāhmaṇam almost totally differing from the Brāhmaṇams of other rescensions. A few Samhitās have several Brāhmaṇams attached to them. According to Indian tradition, the redaction of the Vedas was done at various times by various persons, called Vyāsas, twenty-eight of whom are referred to in Vishṇu Purāṇam, III. iii. This indicates that a considerable period elapsed between the composition of the bulk of the Mantras and their compilation in Samhitā form. The Yajur Veda Samhitā is a collection of prose formulas and of hymns and parts of hymns in the order in which they were required for use in various sacrifices as performed in a later age and intended to be recited by a class of priests called Adhvaryus, who did all the manual work of the sacrificial rites. The Sāma Veda Samhitā contains hymns intended to be sung in the course of the Soma sacrifice by the singing priests or Udgātās. The Mantras of the Rig Veda Samhitā were collected for use by the invoking priests, called Hotās; but as the recitations by the Hotās were not so definitely fixed as those of the Adhvaryus and as the Hotās were required to recite long selections suited to the nature of each sacrificial rite (A. B. ii. 17, iv. 7), the Rig Veda Samhitā, especially, in its books II—VII, does not follow the order of the rites of any particular sacrifice, but its Mantras are arranged according to their traditional authorship. The Samhitā of the Atharva Veda was not compiled for use in public rites but contains hymns to be used in domestic rites. The Samhitās of all the Vedas except the Yajur Veda consist of Sūktams, each Sūktam or hymn containing a number of Mantras, varying in number from one to over one hundred. In some of these Sūktams the Mantras follow each other in the order in which they were probably composed, but in some others (*e.g.* R. V. iv. 18) the Mantras are disconnected, out of context and loosely strung together. Many Mantras and Sūktams are repeated in more than one Samhitā and many others are found in only one. Prose formulas are peculiar to the Yajur Veda and a few prose Sūktams are found in the Atharva Veda.

The language of the Mantras was the literary form of the speech of the people among whom they were composed. These people were of various tribes and spoke many dialects (A. V. xii. 1. 45.) One of these dialects, probably the one spoken by the higher classes of the tribe which lived in the region near the Sarasvatī was conventionalized and adopted as the language of the hymns. Some writers call the Vedic language the vernacular of the ancient people of the Punjab valley. This is not true, for there must have been various dialectical differences between the speeches of contiguous tribes as there is everywhere on the earth; and moreover the language of literature, all the world over, differs from the actual speech of men and women. It is but primitive ballads that are in the spoken idiom of any tribe, and the Mantras are not the simple ballads of love or war sung by a primitive people; but they are composed in an artificial style, full of archaisms and poetic constructions, and complicated, well-defined metrical forms of which there are sixty in the Rig Veda Samhitā and under the influence of a fully developed literary convention. The Vedic language was a "caste-language," a "scholastic dialect of a class," employing forms of different linguistic periods, "an artificially archaic dialect, handed down from one generation to the other within the class of priestly singers"(Macdonnel.Sansk.Lit. p. 20). The extraordinary care with which the musical accent (svara) of the Mantras was preserved in their recitation is another proof that the Vedic language was a "sacred" dialect and not a vernacular. This Vedic language is one of a group of allied languages, called Indo-Germanic, forms of which are used to-day for speech and for writing by the various races inhabiting Europe, Armenia, Persia and Northern India. Hence some people are of opinion that the ancient Vedic language was developed out of dialects spoken by hordes of invading tribes who poured into the valley of the Indus in the commencement of the age of the Mantras and who wiped out the pre-existing population. But the Mantras do not contain any traces of traditions of such an invasion or the remotest allusion to any foreign country which was the first home of these tribes or recollections of the route through which they came. But in whatever way this language came into India, whether it was brought by tribes who invaded the land so long before the age of the Mantras that at the time of their composition, all memory of such invasion was lost or whether it drifted into the country in the wake of the peaceful intercourse between Indian and foreign tribes and ousted the earlier dialects of Northern India on account of its intrinsic merits, the Vedic language bears marks on it of a pretty long growth since it parted from its allied forms. The vowel system of the Vedic language is much simpler and its consonant system more developed than those of the parent Indo-Germanic or of its European branches. A large portion of the vocabulary of the Vedic tongue is not found in the allied languages and must have been picked up in India; and even in matters of syntax and sentence-structure, it underwent special developments on Indian soil.

The Mantras were not all composed at one time. The Samhitās contain, to quote the words of one of the Mantras, "ancient, intermediate and modern hymns." (R. V. iii. 32. 13.) Worshippers, born of old and the men of the middle and later ages are also, often, referred to (R. V. vi. 21. 5, v. 42. 6, etc). These hymns were compiled more than 3000 years ago into Samhitās for use in rites, but they were composed in the II millennium B.C. The authors of the hymns, called Rishis, composed them for the purpose of invoking the help of gods in events that immediately interested them, to secure success in impending battles (R. V. i. 100, ii. 30, etc.) to meet the necessities of the ordinary incidents of daily life of men and women (A. V. xix. 4), to avert drought (R. V. v. 68), to help to raise crops (A. V. vi. 142), to enable them to live a "hundred autums" till their sons became fathers in their turn (R. V. i. 89. 9), to satisfy all possible wants (A. V. xv. 9), and to escape all kinds of dangers and difficulties (A. V. xix. 7). They served to drive out of the body the demons that caused fever (A. V. v. 22) jaundice (A. V. i. 22), and other diseases (A. V. iii. 31) to bewitch and kill enemies (A. V. iv. 18), to stimulate love in indifferent lovers (A. V. vi. 130), or unresponsive sweethearts (A. V. iii. 25), to charm animals (A. V. iv. 3) to secure wives (R. V. ix. 67. 9—11), and children (R. V. viii. 35. 10) and to enable all undertakings to succeed (A. V. vii. 16). As the Mantras relate both to the public and the domestic life of the people, a fairly accurate picture of it during the age of their composition can be constructed from the Samhitās. In doing so, scholars have generally treated the Rig Veda Samhitā as referring to a state of society earlier than that to which the Atharva Veda Samhitā belongs. It may be that the compilation of the Atharva Veda Mantras into a Samhitā was made later than the compilation of the Rig Veda Samhitā, but this cannot be any evidence of the priority of the state of society referred to in the Rig Veda Mantras. Both Samhitās contain older hymns as well as later ones and though a few old hymns can be differentiated from a few late ones by linguistic or other considerations, the bulk of the Mantras belong to the same age, that which we have designated "the age of the Mantras;" besides they refer to the same stage of civilization. The Rig Veda Samhitā contains mostly Mantras required in rites for promoting the interests of tribes as a whole or of wealthy men who could pay for the celebration of costly sacrifices; the Atharva Veda Samhitā, on the other hand, mostly contains Mantras to be used in the simpler home rites of the ordinary men and is on that account ever more useful to the historian than the Rig Veda Samhitā. This age is usually called the Vedic age.

Since, according to Indian usage, the word, 'Veda' covers both the Mantras and the Brāhmaṇams, the phrase, 'the age of the Mantras' is more accurate than the phrase, 'Vedic age.'

During this age, numerous dialects of three distinct families of speech were spoken in India. Of these, the Indo-Germanic dialects, of one of which the Vedic language was the literary counterpart has already been referred to. The Dravidian family which differs from the Indo-Germanic in structure was the second. The Dravidian dialects affected profoundly the sounds, the structure, the idiom and the vocabulary of the former and the differences already alluded to between the Vedic language and its hypothetic parent, called Indo-Germanic or its European descendants, Greek, Latin, etc., are due to the influence of the Dravidian dialects of India. In the course of its growth in India, on account of the constant influence of the Dravidian tongues, this language lost the subjunctive mood, many infinitive forms, and several noun-declensions, forgot its richly varied system of real verb tenses and adopted turns of expressions peculiar to the Dravidian idiom. Compare Sansk. kritavān, Tamil s'eydavan, iti chet, after an assertion to indicate a condition, Telugu aṅṭe, kiñcha, Telugu mariyunu, tasya krite dattam instead of tasmai dattam, Telugu, vāni koraku ichchinadi, etc. The third Indian family of languages is the Muṇḍā; this does not seem to have affected the growth of the Vedic language so much as the Dravidian. In modern times the Indo-Germanic dialects are spoken in North India, the Dravidian in Southern India and the Muṇḍā dialects in the Chota Nagpur plateau and adjoining hills and jungles. But in the age of the Mantras, their areas of prevalence were probably not so sharply divided from one another as now. The Muṇḍā dialects never gave birth to a literature; the Dravidian literature was born more than a millennium after the age of the Mantras, so that for a history of the Indian people in this age, we have got the Vedic Mantras as our only source of information. But yet, we know that the Dravidian speaking races of India traded with the ancient Chaldeans, before the Vedic language found its way into India. Indian teak was found in the ruins of Ur (now Mugheir) and must have reached there from India in the fourth millennium B.C., when it was the seaport of Babylonia and the capital of Sumerian kings (Sayce: Hib. Lect. p. 137). The gold, pearls and spices mentioned in Assyrian inscriptions of the XIV Cen. B. C. (Rawlinson: VI, Or. Mon. p. 33), were probably exported from India, the only country where, so far as we know, they were produced. Peacocks, (called in Hebrew tukīyīm, from tokai, its old Tamil name), were exported to the court of Solomon (962 B. C. — 930 B. C.) *via* ports on the Persian Gulf (Hommel: Civil-East. p. 92). In an old Babylonian list of clothes occurs the word sindhu, meaning muslin (the s'adin of the old Testament, sindon of the Greeks) and all scholars are agreed that this meant Indian cloth (Sayce: Hib. Lect. p. 138). This cloth did not reach Babylonia through Persia by land, for in that case "the original *s* would have become *h* in Persian mouths." (*Ib.*) It will be shown later that the tribes among whom the Vedic Mantras were composed knew of the sea and sea voyages by report and not at first hand and therefore this export trade was carried on by the Dravidian speaking races. This inference is strengthened by the facts that the Dravidian name for ships (ōḍa) is an original word and not borrowed from Sanskrit, that there exists to-day around the southern coasts of India many primitive tribes of sailors speaking Tamil and that the earliest Tamil books that we have, refer to sea-trade in the beginning of the Christian era as an ordinary occupation of the people. The Greek name for rice, (o r y z a) was borrowed straight from the Tamil a r i s' i and not through its Sanskritized from v r ī h i ; and Greek p e p e r i is the Dravidian p i p p a l i, long pepper. The Sanskrit name of pearl, m u k t ā is from the Tamil m u t t u, its name in the land where it is dived for ; sandal was another product of South India, which travelled with its name to places far from its original name.

The Vedic Mantras mention the names of about forty tribes who inhabited the regions known to their composers. The centre of this region was the district round the Sarasvatī, south of the modern Ambāla. The westernmost tribe referred to is that of the Gandhāras (R.V. i. 126. 7, A. V. v. 22.14) who lived in what we now call Afghanistan and Baluchistan, and the most eastern, the Kīkaṭas (R.V. iii. 53.14) Magadhas and Angas (A. V. v. 22.14) of South Behar. The Himavanta (Himalaya) mountains (R.V. x. 121. 4) formed its northern boundary and one of its peaks, Trikakud (now Trikoṭa) is referred to (A.V. iv. 9.9). But the Vindhya mountains towards the south are not mentioned in the Mantras, though that there must have been intercourse between North and South India is proved by the fact that pearls, a South Indian product, are mentioned in the Mantras often, and besides pearls, gold, too, was probably got from Southern India, where there exist so many traces of ancient gold diggings. The elephants frequently referred to in the Mantras, must have been from the Vindhyan regions as much as from the Himalayan. Peafowls (m a y ū r a) mentioned in R.V. i. 191-14 were probably imported, with their name too, from South India.

In the North-western part of India, in the districts in the midst of which ran the Sarasvatī river lived those tribes among whom the Mantras were composed. Scholars have given the name "Aryas" to these tribes and till recently also applied the name to a supposed Aryan race which sent successive swarms of invaders to India, Persia, Greece, Italy, Germany, France, Britain and civilized those lands in pre-historic times. But the progress of anthropology has proved the invasion and civilization of Europe by the "Aryans" to be a myth. Scholars yet cling to the theory of an "Aryan" race, so far as India is concerned; but the evidence of the Vedic Mantras does not lend any support to the theory. The "Aryas" and "Dasyus" or "Dāsas" are referred to in them, but not as indicating different races. One solitary word, a n ā s a which occurs in one solitary passage, R.V. v. 29.10 is quoted to prove that the Dasyus were a flat-nosed race. Sāyaṇa, the Hindu commentator on the Vedas explains the word to be a n - ā s a, mouthless, devoid of (good) speech; but Max Müller explains the word as a - n ā s a, noseless and on this interpretation are built theories about the racial characteristics of the aboriginal races of India! Sāyana's interpretation seems the correct one, because the Dasyus are called in two other passages (R.V. i. 174.2, v. 32.8) m r i d h r a v ā c h a, of injurious speech, a phrase applied in two other passages (R.V. vii. 6.3, vii. 18.13) to Paṇis, beings similar to the Dasyus. But even if Max Müller's interpretation were right, it seems absurd to base ethnological theories on one solitary word and that applied to Dasyus by their enemies, all the more so as the word Dasyu is applied indifferently to men and to demons and in the particular passage, which means, "Thou [Indra] didst detach one wheel for the Sun; the other thou didst set free to go for Kutsa's sake. Thou hast with thy weapon smitten the a n ā s a Dasyus; in their abode thou hast beaten down the injurious speaking" (R. V. v. 29. 10), the Dasyus are certainly demons. A word K r i s h ṇ a, which occurs in R. V. i. 101. 1, i. 130. 8, ii. 20. 7, iv. 16. 13, viii. 62. 8, viii. 85. 15 and ix. 41. 1, is interpreted 'black' and on the strength of this, the Dasyus are described to have been a black race and the "Aryans," therefore a white race. But these passages have also been interpreted to refer to (1) black demons, (2) black clouds, (3) Krishṇa, a demon and a foe of Indra, by commentators Indian and Western. Similarly the word a s i k n i, which occurs in R. V. vii. 5. 3 and ix. 73. 5, is interpreted as (1) "dark races" or (2) "powers of darkness." On these passages in the Mantras, all of doubtful import, is based the far-reaching theory of the white "Aryan race" displacing the black Dasyu races of India!

Of late, an attempt has been made to support this theory of an "Aryan race" by anthropometrical considerations. "The Aryan type...is marked by a relatively long (dolichocephalic) head; a straight finely-cut (leptorrhine) nose; a long, symmetrically narrow face; well-developed regular features and a high facial angle. The stature is fairly high......and the general build of the figure well-proportioned and slender rather than massive" (Haddon: S t u d y o f M a n, p. 103). This race moved into India, it is supposed about 1700 B.C. "perhaps associated with Turki tribes" (Haddon: W a n d. R a c e s, p. 21) "by tribes and families, without any disturbance of their social order" at a time when, it is supposed, the North-western frontier of India was "open to the slow advance of family or tribal migration" (I m p. G a z. I n d. i. p. 302). The previous inhabitants of the fertile valleys of the five rivers vanished before the advancing "Aryans" so as not to pollute the "Aryan" type and as soon as the "Aryans" had moved into the Punjab, the North-west frontier was "closed" to further migration by the hand of God. Supposing all these miracles took place in the remote past, we know from subsequent history that innumerable races poured in to India through the North-western passes, that Persians, European Greeks, Bactrians, Scythians, Huns, Afghans, Tartars and Moguls have all contributed to a welter of races in the Punjab and that hence the Punjabi cannot be held to possess the characteristics of the pure "Aryan" stock of 1700 B.C.

A careful examination of the Mantras where the words Arya, Dāsa and Dasyu occur, indicates that they refer not to race but to cult. These words occur mostly in the Rig Veda Samhitā, where 'Arya' occurs about 33 times in Mantras which contain 1,53,972 words on the whole. This rare occurrence is itself a proof that the tribes that called themselves "Aryas" were not invading tribes that conquered the country and exterminated the people. For an invading tribe would naturally boast of its achievements constantly. The word 'Dāsa' occurs about 50 times and 'Dasyus' about 70 times. The comparatively more frequent occurrence of these two words is due to their use in some of these passages, the first in the sense of slave or servant, and the second of robber ; where these words are not used in these meanings they refer either to demons or to men who were opposed to the Aryas. The word Arya occurs 22 times in hymns to Indra and 6 times in hymns to Agni ; Dāsa, 45 times in hymns to Indra, twice in hymns to Agni and Dasyu 50 times in hymns to Indra and 9 times in hymns to Agni. The constant association of these words with Indra clearly proves that Arya meant a worshipper of Indra (and Agni) and Dāsa or Dasyu meant either demons opposed to Indra or the people that worshipped these demons. That the Aryas worshipped Indra and he helped them in their cattle-raids and other quarrels is the constant burden of the Mantras where the word Ārya occurs. The Aryas offered oblations to Indra, through Agni and next to Indra, Agni was their great helper (R. V. vii. 18. 7, viii. 92. 1, etc). The Dasyus or Dāsas were those who were opposed to the Indra-Agni cult and are so explicitly described in those passages where human Dasyus are clearly meant. They are a v r a t a, without (the Ārya) rites (R. V. i. 51. 8, 9, i. 132. 4, iv. 41. 2, vi. 14. 3), a p a v r a t a, (R. V. v. 42. 9), a n y a v r a t a, of different rites (R. V. viii. 59. 11, x. 22. 8), a n a g n i t r a, fireless (R. V. v. 189. 3), ayajyu, ayajvāna, non-sacrificers (R. V. i. 131. 4, 4, i. 33. 4, viii. 59. 11), a b r a h m ā, without prayers (or also not having Brāhmaṇa priests) (R. V. iv. 16. 9, x. 105. 8), a n r i c h a ḥ, without Riks (R. V. x. 105. 8), b r a h m a d v i s h a, haters of prayer (or Brāhmaṇas), (R V. v. 42. 9), and a n i n d r a, without Indra, despisers of Indra, (R. V. i. 133. i, v. 2. 3, vii. 18. 6, x. 27. 6, x. 48. 7). "They pour no milky draughts; they heat no cauldron" (R. V. iii. 53. 4). They give no gifts to the Brāhmaṇa (R. V. v. 7. 10). "Men fight the fiend and seek by rites to overcome the riteless foe" (R. V. vi. 14. 3). Their worship was but enchantment (R. V. iii. 34. 3), sorcery (R. V. iv. 16. 9), unlike the sacred law of fire-worship (R. V. v. 12. 2), wiles and magic (R. V. v. 31. 7, vi. 20. 4), godless arts of magic (R. V. vii. i. 10). Contrariwise the Aryans were those who worshipped Indra and Agni. [Indra-Agni], "when two great hosts, arrayed against each other, meet clothed with brightness, in the fierce encounter, stand ye beside the godly, smite the godless, and still assist the men who press the soma." (R. V. vii. 93. 5). "The man who, sacrificing, strives to win the heart of deities will conquer those who will not" (R. V. viii. 31. 15. 18). Thus a complete analysis of the references in the Vedic passages shows that the difference between the Aryas and the Dasyus was not one of race but of cult. Nor was there any difference of culture between the Arya and the Dasyu ; according to the hymns composed for performing the Arya rites, the Dasyus lived in cities (R. V. i. 53. 8, i. 103. 3) and under kings the names of many of whom are mentioned. They possessed "accumulated wealth" (R. V. viii. 40. 6) in the form of cows, horses and chariots (R .V. ii. 15. 4) which though kept in "hundred gated cities," (R. V. x. 99. 3), Indra seized and gave away to his worshippers, the Aryas, (R. V. i. 176. 4). The Dasyus were wealthy (R. V. i. 33. 4) and owned property "in the plains and on the hills" (R. V. x. 69. 6). They were "adorned with their array of gold and jewels" (R. V. i. 33. 8). They owned many castles (R. V. i. 33. 13, viii. 17. 14). The Dasyu demons and the Arya gods alike lived in gold, silver and iron castles (S. Y. S. vi. 23, A. V. v. 28. 9, R. V. ii. 20. 8). Indra overthrew for his worshipper, Divodāsa, frequently mentioned in the hymns, a "hundred stone castles" (R. V. iv. 30. 20) of the Dasyus. Agni, worshipped by the Arya, gleaming in behalf of him, tore and burnt the cities of the fireless Dasyus. (R. V. vii. 5. 3). Brihaspati broke the stone prisons in which they kept the cattle raided from the Aryas (R. V. iv. 28. 5,x. 67. 3). The Dasyus owned chariots and used them in war like the Aryas and had the same weapons as the Aryas (R. V. viii. 24. 27, iii. 30. 5, ii. 15. 4). The distinction indicated by "Arya" and "Dasyu" was purely a difference of cult and not of race or culture. Some, at least, if not all the people called

Dasyu spoke ancient forms of the Dravidian or Muṇḍā dialects. Their worship probably resembled that of tribes who have not been affected by the Arya cult even to-day and who speak Dravidian or Muṇḍā dialects. They killed buffaloes and goats in honour of their Gods, and let the blood of the victims flow on their fireless altars; they did not throw any part of the sacrificial animal into fire nor did they accompany their sacrifice with prayers old or new. The Arya method of sacrifice must have appeared a strange rite to the Dasyus who are said to have frequently disturbed the Arya rites and drunk the oblations intended for the Arya gods. (R. V. v. 32. 8, vii. 18. 6). Indeed according to Indian tradition throughout the ages, Dasyu and Arya have been understood respectively as enemies and advocates of the fire-cult. The Nirukta defines a Dasyu to be the destroyer of rites (Nir. vii. 23). Sāyaṇa defines Aryas to be *stotārah*, those that sing hymns (Comm. on R.V. R. V. i. 103), *karmayuktāni*, practising fire-rites, (Comm. on R. V. vi. 22. 10), *karmānushṭhātritvena sreshṭāni*, most excellent through doing fire-rites (Comm. on R.V. vi. 33. 3) and Dasyus to be *anushṭhātrīṇam upakshapayitārah s'atravah*, enemies who destroy the observers of fire-rites, (Comm. on R. V. i. 51. 8), *karmaṇām upakshapayitrīh*, destroyers of rites (Comm. on R.V. vi. 25. 2), *karmahīnāh*, riteless (comm. R. V. vi. 60. 6).

Let us consider for a while the implications of the facts and arguments adduced in the previous paragraphs. The Aryan invasion of India is a theory invented to account for the existence of an Indo-Germanic language in North India. In tracing the history of India after this theoretical event, scholars treat of India as if the previous inhabitants were so few and so devoid of stamina or of culture as to be practically effaced by the invaders or steadily driven to the East. On the contrary, in one hymn the Dasyus are said to have been driven "westward" (R. V. vii. 6. 3), as the result of a battle. The truth is that, when the dialects corresponding to the Vedic speech arrived in India, the country was not a barren waste, but its rich valleys were filled with a teeming population, speaking dialects of the Dravidian and Muṇḍā languages. They were not primitive tribes but tilled the ground and raised crops of various kinds, *e.g.*, rice, sesamum, etc. They worked in metals, the Dravidian name for a smith, k a r u m ā, from which the vedic k a r m ā r a is probably borrowed, meant a smelter; their artificers made ornaments of gold, pearls and probably of precious stones for their kings and princes; they built chariots, the like of which are seen to-day, attached to temples and used for processions of Gods. They traded with foreign countries and exported teak, peacocks, spices, pearls and probably woven cloth. The Dravidian names of things and operations connected with all these arts of peace are native and not foreign (*i.e.*, borrowed from Sanskrit). The question has not yet been investigated, but on enquiry it will most probably turn out that many Sanskrit words connected with these arts were borrowed from the Dravidian. It is not surprising, therefore, that this Indo-Germanic language was profoundly affected when it spread among the people of ancient India, that it shed some of its vowels, Indo-Germanic *a*, *e*, *o*, all being levelled down to one uniform *a*, that it developed new consonants, *e.g.*, the sibilants, *s*, *s'*, *sh*, hopelessly confused in the pronunciation of Sanskrit in various parts of India and that its grammar was slowly but surely modified. Whether this language spread in the wake of peaceful intercourse or was suddenly planted in India in the remote past by a small army of invaders, there could not have been any appreciable racial disturbance and, in any case, the Dravidian speaking races were sufficiently civilized and numerous to absorb completely the foreigners and enrich their speech with words relating to the professions which were highly developed among themselves. Along with the Dasyus, the Vedic hymns mention the Paṇis. Paṇi (*cf.* Vāṇia, bania) meant a trader and was probably the name of a Dravidian speaking trading tribe which refused to accept the fire-cult.

It has been pointed out that the special feature of the worship of the Aryas was that oblations to their Gods, major and minor, were offered through fire and were accompanied by recitations of hymns. They believed that the man in whose house Agni dwelt as guest could, by sacrifice, conquer mortals, that aided by him they could secure victory in battles, gain wealth and defeat plotters of evil (R. V. v. 3. 5. 7). But sacrifice unaccompanied by prayer was inefficacious. "With song will we conquer the men who sing no hymns: not easily art thou [Indra] pleased with prayerless sacrifice" (R. V. x. 105, 8). "No juices pressed without a prayer have pleased him" (R. V. vii. 26, 1). Whence came this fire-cult, which was unknown to the speakers of the Dravidian and Muṇḍa dialects that prevailed in India before the arrival of the Vedic language, whether it came in the wake of this language or was evolved on Indian soil afterwards are questions impossible of solution at present. The existence of a form of the fire-cult associated with Zoroastrianism in ancient Media does not throw any light on these questions, because (1) the existence of the teaching of Zoroaster cannot be traced beyond the eighth or ninth century B. C. and the Indian fire-cult was very much older ; (2) the fire-god of the Indians was called Agni and that of the Zoroastrians was Āthar ; if the two had the same source, there is no reason why their names should not have been identical ; (3) there is a very characteristic difference between the fire-cults ; whereas with the Indian, all oblations, whether derived from the vegetable or the animal worlds were thrown into fire, with the Zoroastrians, fire was so holy that animal substances would pollute it, to prevent which a bit of the skin or hair of the slaughtered sacrificial victim was shown to the fire and thrown aside, and (4) the Zoroastrian fire was kept up for many years and if it went out, had to be renewed with great ceremony, whereas the Indian sacrificial fire was produced when wanted by attrition. Besides there are distinct references in the Mantras to the beginnings of the fire-cult in India. In several Mantras, the Angirases are said to have instituted the fire-rites. "Our sires with lauds burst even the firm-set fortress, yea, the Angirases, with roar, the mountain. They made for us a way to reach high heaven, they found us day, light, day's sign, beams of morning. They established order, made his service fruitful" (R. V. i. 71. 2 3, *vide* also R. V. v. 11. 6). The Bhrigus seem to have also been early institutors of sacrifices. "The Bhrigus established thee [Agni] among mankind for men, like as a treasure, bounteous, easy to invoke ; Thee, Agni, as a herald and choice-worthy guest, as an auspicious friend to the celestial race" (R. V. i. 58. 6). Manu is frequently mentioned as the institutor of fire-rites (R. V. i. 14. 11, i. 36. 19, etc.). Atharvā and Dadhyak were other early establishers of the fire-cult (R.V. i. 80. 16, 83. 5). Besides mythical men, races too are referred to as starting the fire-cult. "Then, when the Arya tribes chose as invoking priest Agni, the wonder-worker, and the hymn rose up" (A. V. xviii. 1. 21). The Bharatas, one of the chief tribes mentioned in the Mantras, seem to have been the first to adopt the fire-rite, because Agni is called Bhārata in several Mantras (R. V. ii. 7. 1. 5, iv. 25. 4, vi. 16. 19). Agni is said to shine specially for the Bharatas (R.V. v. 11. 1, vi. 16. 45); the Bharatas set Agni in the place of prayer, between the Sarasvatī and the Drishadvatī (R. V. iii. 23. 4), their Agni is far famed (R. V. vii. 8. 4); in later days, this tribe gave its name to the whole of India.

The people that inhabited the Punjab and the upper Gangetic valley in the age of the Mantras were not roving hordes of pastoral tribes, but lived in an organized society. They were ruled by kings, many of whom are mentioned by name; the most interesting are Ikshvāku (R. V. x. 60. 4) and S'antanu (x. 98. 1), and the doughty warriors, Sudās and Trasadasyu, frequently referred to. Kings resided in forts (p ū r) supported by a "thousand columns" (R. V. ii. 41. 5, v. 62. 6) and provided with a "thousand" doors (R. V. vii. 88. 5), where they sat on a throne (g a r t a), "of iron columns, decked with gold" (R. V. v. 62. 7) and held court arrayed in golden mail (h i r a ṇ y a y a d r ā p i) and shining robes, surrounded by ministers (v e s'a s a), spies (s p a s' a) (R. V. i. 25. 10, 13), heralds proclaiming their glory (R. V. x. 40. 3), courtiers extolling them (R. V. i. 173. 10) and messengers (d ū t a) to convey their commands (R. V x. 123. 6). Some of these phrases occur in descriptions of Gods, but we may be sure that the life of the Gods was modelled on that of mortal kings; as the S'atapatha Brāhmaṇam naively puts it, "the course pursued among the Gods is in accordance with that pursued among men" (I. iii. 1. 1). Kings attended assemblies clad in robes of state (n i r ṇ i j a, R. V. ix. 71. 1). Some form of carpet was spread under their seats (*Ib.*) They sat surrounded by noble friends (R. V. iii. 55. 21), chief of whom were skilful chariot-builders, ingenious workers in metals (artizans not being in those days a despised caste), king-makers (r ā j a k ṛ i t a), charioteers (s ū t a) and leaders of hosts (g r ā m a ṇ ī, A. V. iii. 5. 6, 7). Public questions were discussed in assemblies, but the will of the king of course prevailed, as Indra's will is said to be "like a sovran in assembly" (R. V. iv. 21. 2). On state occasions and at other times too, bards went in the train of the kings praising them (R. V. iii. 54.14, ix. 10.3). Kings were autocratic and their anger was dreaded. "Let the fury of kings fall on others, not on me," prays a ṛishi (A. V. vi. 40.2). Royal palaces were built of wood and more or less primitive adumbrations of the wooden palace of Chandragupta at Pāṭaliputra in the IV century B. C. Fire is said to rend "forts as age consumes a garment" (R. V. iv. 16. 13). But stone castles (R. V. iv. 30. 20) are mentioned, as well as stone walls (A. V. v. 10. 7); these forts, though called s'a t a b h u j i, (R. V. i. 166·8, vii. 15. 4), *i.e.*, having hundred concentric walls could not have been elaborate structures, for there are now no relics of stone architecture of any earlier age than the 5th century B. C. The roofs of palaces were supported by wooden pillars on which were carved figures of unrobed girls (R. V. iv. 32. 23.) Iron castles (ā y a s ī h p u r a h) are referred to (R. V. vii. 3. 7, vii. 15. 14, vii. 95. 1, viii. 89.8) and were probably stockades of sāl wood, faced with iron. Kings rode on elephants (A. V. iii. 22. 4), well decorated (R. V. ix. 57. 3), or chariots decked with mother-of-pearl (k r i s' a n a, R. V. i. 35. 4) and gold (R. V. i. 66. 3) and drawn by "well-fed horses" (R. V. iv. 37. 4.) The king's charioteer (s ū t a) was the master of the horse and was an intimate friend of his employer. (A. V. iii. 5. 7). The charioteer sat on the right of the chariot and the king on a chair in the left: when the king fought from a chariot, he stood on the left (savyashṭhā. A. V. viii. 8. 23, R. V. vi. 20.9). Kings married many wives (R. V. vii. 18. 2), the principal consort, called Mahishī, ruled the royal household (A. V. ii. 36. 3); Agni, shining on high, rich in light, from whom riches and strength come to the worshipper is compared to a king's Mahishī (R. V. v. 25. 7). The word vadhri, emasculated men, occurs in R.V. i. 33.6 and royal wives were probably guarded by them. One hymn speaks of Rodasī "moving in seclusion, like a man's wife." (R. V. i. 167. 3) and this has been interpreted by Sāyana to refer to women in a harem. Kings maintained royal priests and gave them lavish gifts (R. V. vii. 18. 22-24). Kings were elected by the people (vis', A. V. iii. 4. 2), *i.e.* the man chosen from the royal family by the "king-makers" was acclaimed rājā by the assembled clansmen. He was then consecrated. Standing on a tiger-skin, a "tiger on a tiger-skin" (A. V. iv. 8. 4), the priest sprinkled (abhisheka) on him water consecrated with mantras (A. V. iv. 8. 5) and recited prayers for the king's long life and prosperity (R. V. x. 173). The king then gave the abhīvarta oblation to the Gods, to reign without a rival as sovereign of his tribes (R. V. x. 174). Kings levied "abundant tribute" (bali, A. V. iii. 4. 3) from the rich; so much so, that Agni is said "to eat the woods as a king eats the rich (R. V. i. 65. 4). These tributes must have been heavy because the heaven-world is described as a place where no tribute (s'ulka) is paid by the weak to the mighty (A. V. iii. 29. 3). Kings of various grades are mentioned in the hymns, the rājaka being inferior to a r ā j ā (R. V. viii. 21. 18), and s v a r ā ṭ, independent king (R. V. ii. 28. 1) and s a m r ā ṭ, paramount king (R. V. iv. 19. 2) being superior to him. Below the rājaka or petty prince was the town-king (p ū r p a t i, R. V. i. 173. 10). Public affairs, religious and political, were managed by local assemblies (s a b h ā, s a m i t i, A. V. vii. 12. 1) and speakers in these assemblies sought the help of spells and magic herbs to stimulate their eloquence in debate (p r ā s′) and overcome their rival debaters (p r a t i p r ā s′i t a) (A. V. ii. 27) and secure unanimous support from the assembled tribesmen (A. V. vii. 12). In a hymn to j ñ ā n a m, knowledge, a successful debater is lauded. "All friends are joyful in the friend who comes in triumph, having conquered in assembly. He is their blame-averter, food-provider, prepared is he and fit for deed of vigour" (R. V. x. 71. 10).

Wealthy men, "whose chariot-seat comes laden with wealth and bright with gold, lightly, with piercing axle-ends, like two ranks of heroes ranged for fight," performed sacrifices and gave liberal presents to priests (R. V. vi. 47. 21—26). The names of some of these lords (m a g h a v ā), Duhs′īma Prithavāna, Rāma, Vena, Tānva, Pārthya, Māyava, occur in R. V. x. 93. 14-15. Several other names are found in other Mantras. The nobles possessed chariots and horses; the horses were "long-maned, whose bodies fill the girths" (R. V. i. 10. 3). They were fed with roasted grain (d h ā n a R. V. iii. 35. 7, iii. 52. 7) and kept in stables (A. V. iii. 15. 8). They were well-groomed (R. V. i. 60. 5) with a brush or comb called m ṛ i k s h a (R. V. viii. 55. 3). The nobles drove in "lightly rolling chariots" (R. V. i. 183. 3), "drawn by four trained horses decked with pearls" (R. V. vii. 18. 23), champing bit and bridle (y a m a s ā n a ā s ā, (R. V. viii

3. 4). Priests flocked round liberal lords, chanting prayers for prosperity and performing magical rites for killing their human and demon foes and received rewards constantly. Asaṅga, a prince of the Yadu tribe, husband of S'as'vatī, was changed into a woman by the gods and Medhyātithi by his prayers restored him to manhood. When S'as'vatī anu asya sthūram dadris'e purastāt anastha ūruh avarambhamāṇah, Medhyātithi was given "ten bright-hued oxen, like lotus-stalks standing out of a lake." (R. V. viii. 1. 34). Some rich men were liberal, others not; the hymn to liberality (R. V. x. 117), says: "The gods have not ordained hunger to be our destruction. Even those who are full-fed are over-taken by various forms of death. The prosperity of the liberal man never decays; while the illiberal finds no comforter...He is no friend who bestows nothing on his friend who waits upon him, seeking sustenance. Let every one depart from such a man,—his house is no home,—and look out for some one else who is liberal, even though he be a stranger." (*Ib.* 2. 4). The rich profligate "bathed in milk" (R. V. i. 104. 3), decked himself "for show, with glittering ornaments, and bound his breasts with chains of gold for beauty" (R. V. i. 64. 4), gleamed with armlets "as the heavens are decked with stars" (R. V. ii. 34. 2) and thus "flung away his treasure (R. V. i. 104. 5) and caused riches "to revolve, from one hand to another, like the wheels of a chariot" (R. V. x. 117. 5). The bulk of the people were poor and borrowed at usurious rates of interest (R. V. viii. 55. 10) and repaid their debts in eight or sixteen instalments (R. V. viii. 47. 17, A. V. vi. 46. 3). There is also a reference to paying "debt from debt," *i.e.*, compounding of old debts with new ones, so common to-day among professional money-

lenders. There are two hymns in the Atharva Veda for securing release from debts (vi. 117. 119). Famines prevailed not infrequently (R. V. iii. 8. 2, iii. 53. 15, viii. 18. 11, viii. 55. 14, x. 43. 10), when the starving poor, desirous of food courted the man with a store of sustenance; the "lean beggar craving food" (R. V. x. 117. 2. 3) ate even poisonous plants, after washing off the poison with water (A. V. iv. 7. 1. 3) and people died of starvation (A. V. iv. 17. 6) during famines.

The chief occupation of the people was agriculture. They ploughed the ground, the plough (s ī r a, R. V. x. 101. 3, l ā ṅ g a l a, A. V. ii. 8. 4) being drawn by two oxen (R. V. x. 106 2) fastened to the yoke with hempen or leather traces (R. V. iii. 17. 3, R. V. x. 101. 3) and driven with a goad (ā j a n ī, A. V. iii. 25. 5, R. V. iv. 57. 4). The ploughshare (p a v i r a) was made of iron, (A. V. iii. 17. 3), which supplanted the older ploughshare made of k h a d i r a wood (A. V. v. 6. 6). The ploughmen (k ī n ā s' a) sang merrily to the steers (R. V. viii. 20. 19) while ploughing; they bedewed the furrow, s ī t ā, with ghī and honey before sowing (A. V. iii. 17. 9). The fields were watered by means of irrigation canals (k u l y ā, R. V. iii. 45. 3, i r i ṇ ā, A. V. iv. 15. 12) from wells or lakes (A. V. i. 3. 7, iii. 13. 9, R. V. iii. 45. 3, vii. 49. 2, 4, x. 43. 7) or by raising water from wells by means of wooden or metal buckets tied to a rope pulled round a stone pulley (a s' m a c h a k r a m R. V. x. 101. 5. 7). They kept away birds from robbing them of the growing corn by uttering loud cries (R. V. x. 68. 1). They reaped the fields with sickles (s ṛ i ṇ ī, A. V. iii. 17. 2, R. V. x. 101. 3, p a r s' u. A. V. xii. 3. 31) and stacked the sheaves near, leaving three sheaves, to the good goblins (g a n d h a r v a) that guarded the field (A. V. iii. 24. 6). Four sheaves were tied together and hung in the house to propitiate the goddess of the house. (*Ib.*) They threshed them on threshing-floors (k h a l a, R. V. x. 48. 7), winnowed the corn in winnowing baskets (s t h i v i, R. V. x. 27. 15) and then carted it to their homes (R. V. i. 9. 8) and stored it in granaries (R. V. ii. 14. 11). It was measured before being stored, the unit of measure being called k h ā r ī (R. V. iv. 32. 17). Agriculture was followed not merely for providing one's own family with food but as a means of acquiring wealth. For when ploughing was commenced, they recited the mantra "Let the plough, lance-pointed, well-lying, with well-smoothed handle, turn up cow, sheep, an on-going chariot and a plump wench" (A. V. iii. 17. 3). The enemies of the agriculturists were rodents, insects and demons, which were exorcised by means of spells (A. V. vi. 50). A great number of them are named, *e.g.*, t a r d a, s a m a ṅ k a, u p a k v a s a, v a g h ā, but cannot be identified. In the ponds for storing water, the lotus was grown ; lotus-ponds were much desiderated (A. V. v. 17. 6). Fruit is frequently referred to and therefore fruit-gardens were maintained. The poets of this age were not hampered by the rhetorical conventions of a later time with regard to the choice of poetical images and we find that the work of the cultivator furnished them with metaphors. Sacrifice to the gods is figuratively described as agriculture. "Lay on the yokes, and fasten well the traces. Formed is the furrow ; sow the seed within it. Through song may we find hearing fraught with plenty : near to the ripened grain approach the sickle ; wise, through desire of bliss from gods, the skilful bind the traces fast, and lay the yokes on either side. Arrange the buckets in their place : securely fasten on the straps. We will pour forth the well that hath a copious stream, fair-flowing well that never fails" (R. V. x. 101. 3, 5). The allusions to pasture are not so frequent as those to agriculture, cattle-rearing being followed as subsidiary to agriculture. Cowherds (g o p a) took cows out to pasture daily (R. V. x. 19. 4. 5). They drove forth cattle, with a goad (g o o p a s' a), furnished with a steel-pin (R. V. vi. 53. 9), as Indra drives his car to where his worshippers are gathered (R. V. v. 31. 1). On the pasture land the herdsman guarded the cattle, as Indra goes round and round an army in combat and saves the soldier from harm (R. V. vi. 19. 3). He called animals that strayed from the herd, as the sacrificers attract Indra to the place of oblation (R. V. x. 23. 6). He watched the herd as Sūrya surveys the world and living creatures (R. V. vii. 60. 3). On return from pasture, the cows were kept in stalls (g o t r a, R. V. ii. 23. 8, v r a j a, A. V. iii. 11. 5, g o s h ṭ h a, iv. 21. 1) and water-troughs were provided for them in various places (p r a p ā) R. V. vi. 28. 7, d r o ṇ a, R. V. v. 50. 4, p r a p ā ṇ a, A. V. vii. 75. 1). Cows were milked not only by the ladies of the household but also by professional milkers (g o d h u k, A. V. vii. 73. 6) who were "skilful-handed" in milking (A. V. ix. 10. 4). Draught-oxen were castrated; the testes were crushed with claspers (s' l e s h a m ā n a, A. V. iii. 9. 2) or squeezed between two press-stones (A. V. vi. 138. 2). The tips of the horns of oxen were sharpened (R. V. vi. 16. 39) and decked with ornaments (R. V. viii. 54. 10). The ears of cattle were marked on the ear by cutting with a red (*i.e.*, copper) knife (s v a d h i t i) a pair (m i t h u n a) of marks, s t r ī p u m s ā t m a k a m c h i h n a m (as the commentator explains), so that their progeny might be numerous (A. V. vi. 141. 2, R. V. x. 62. 7). They reared also goat and sheep. Fat rams for cooking (R. V. x.

37. 17) and the ewes of Gandhāra famous for their wool (R. V. i. 126. 7) are referred to. Dogs guarded cattle and houses and barked at human thieves (R. V. vii. 55. 3), at wolves worrying sheep (A. V. v, 8. 4, vi. 37. 0) and tigers which "plague the men who are rich in kine" (A. V. iv. 36. 6). Similes derived from the work of the herdsman have already been quoted. In R. V. vi. 24. 4, Indra's various great deeds are said to indicate his divinity, as all "the paths of kine converge homeward" and the ties by which his worshippers are bound to him are ties of love and not of bondage like "the bonds of cord that bind calves." The invocation to the raincloud, imaged as a cow, in a hymn by Dīrghatamas is a beautiful bit of poetry. "I invocate the milch-cow, good for milking so that the milker, deft of hand, may drain her;......she, lady of all treasure, is come here yearning in spirit for her calf, and lowing......The cow hath lowed after her blinking youngling; she licks his forehead, as she lows, to form it. His mouth she fondly calls to her warm udder, and suckles him with milk while gently lowing. He also snorts, by whom encompassed round the cow lows as she clings unto the shedder of the rain. She with her shrilling cries hath humbled mortal man, and, turned to lightning, hath stripped off her covering robe......Fortunate mayst thou be with goodly pasture, and may we also be exceeding wealthy. Feed on the grass, O cow, at every season, and coming hitherward, drink limpid water. Forming the water-floods, the buffalo hath lowed, one-footed, or two-footed or four-footed. she, who hath become eight-footed or hath got nine-feet, the thousand-syllable in the sublimest heaven. From her descend in streams the seas of water; thereby the world's four regions have their being. Thence flows the imperishable flood, and thence

the universe hath life." (R. V. i. 164. 26, 29, 40. 42).

Weaving in cotton and wool was done by men and women (R. V. ii. 3. 6, x. 26. 6). The garment a bridegroom had to wear on the day of marriage was woven by the bride herself with beautiful borders (s i c h) and given to him (A. V. xiv. 2. 51). Weaving was so well-known that numerous poetical metaphors were drawn from this industry. "The wives of the gods wove a hymn to Indra" (R. V. i. 61. 8). "The sacrifice drawn out with threads on every side, stretched by a hundred sacred ministers and one, this do these fathers weave who hitherward are come; they sit beside the warp and cry, weave forth, weave back. The man extends it and the man unbinds it: even to this vault of heaven hath he outspun it. These pegs are fastened to the seat of worship; they made the sāma hymns their weaving-shuttles (t a s a r a) (R. V. x. 130. 1-2). "I know not the warp (t a n t u) and the woof (o t a) I know not" (R. V. vi. 9. 2). Rats, the enemies of weavers, give rise to a simile "Biting cares devour me, as rats devour the weaver's threads (R. V. i. 105. 8). Carpenters made chariots and carts. The chariots were not primitive ones but had wheels with naves, spokes and fellies (n a b h y a, u p a d h i, p r a d h i, R. V. ii. 39. 4). The linch-pin (ā ṇ i) is mentioned in R. V. i. 35. 6. as the emblem of stability. Wood-work included wood-carving. The gods are compared to the forms "well made by an artizan with a knife (s v a d h i t i) in A. V. xii 3. 33, and decorated bowls are referred to in A. V. xix. 49. 8. The carpenters (t a s h t ā) were "skilled craftsmen" (R. V. v. 29. 15) and to their art is frequently compared the skill shown by poets in the composition of hymns. "Men have fabricated (a t a k s h i s h u h) this hymn as a skilful workman fashions a car." (R. V. i. 130. 6).

"Brihaspati brought it forth like a bowl from out the timber" (R. V. x. 68. 8). A poet claims to be able to bend Indra with his song, "as bends a wright his wheel of solid wood" (R. V. vii. 32. 20). Another interesting image derived from the work of the carpenter is found in R. V. i. 105. 18. "A ruddy wolf beheld me once, as I was faring on my path. He, like a carpenter whose back is aching, crouched and slunk away." Boats and ships are frequently referred to and the art of ship-building was so well-known that the sacrificial rite is compared to ship-building (R. V. x. 101. 2). Houses were mostly of wood and were put up by carpenters, who with their mallets (k ū ṭ a m, A. V. viii. 8. 10) made household utensils, ladles (s r u k, j u h ū, d h r u v ā, A. V. xviii. 4. 5.), cups (u p a b h r i t, A. V. xviii. 4. 5), buckets (u d a c h a, A. V. iv. 15. 6), bowls (c h a m a s a m, R. V. iv. 35. 2), etc. of wood. Blacksmiths (k a r m ā r a) made spears (v a s'i), swords (a s i), hatchets (s v a d h i t i) (R. V. i. 162. 10), quoits (k h ā d i, R. V, v. 58. 2), lances (r i s h ṭ i, R. V. viii. 20. 11), axes (paras'u, R. V. vii. 104. 21). quivers (n i s h a ṅ g a, R. V. v. 57. 2), knives for various purposes, including razors (k s h u r a, R. V. i. 166. 10, viii. 4. 6), helmets (s' i p r a, R. V. v. 54. 11), coats of mail (d r ā p i, R. V. ix. 100. 9), sickles (d ā t r a m, R. V. vii. 67. 10), ploughshares (s' u n ā, R. V. iv. 57. 5) pots (g h a r m ā, R. V. v. 30. 5), goads (a ṅ k u s' a, R. V. vii. 17. 10), needles (s ū c h ī, R. V. i. 191. 7), awls (ā r ā, R. V. vi. 53. 5), hatchets for felling trees (k u l i s' a A. V. ii. 12. 3), hooks for shaking fruits off trees (a r i k a, R. V. iii. 45. 4), iron legs for those who had lost their natural ones (R. V. i. 116. 15), iron-forts, i.e., wooden stockades iron-sheathed (R. V. vii. 3. 7); they tipped with iron (R. V. vi. 3. 5) arrows (i s h u) winged with feathers

(R. V. viii 66. 7) and furnished with poisoned tips (A. V. iv. 6). Goldsmiths melted gold and fashioned bright jewels (a ñ j i, R. V. i. 37. 2) such as necklets (n i s h k a, probably garlands of flat circular pieces of gold, corresponding to the wreaths of gold coins now worn, (R V. i. 126. 2), armlets (k h ā d i, R. V. v. 53. 4) anklets (k h ā d i, R. V. v. 54. 11) girdles (k a k s h y ā, R. V. x. 10.13), chains (s r a k, R. V. x. 53. 9) and ornaments for the breast (R. V. viii. 20. 22). They made water-ewers (k a l a s'a m) of gold (R. V. iv. 32. 19) and images (?) of kings. (h i r a ṇ y a s a n d r i s'o r ā j ñ a h, R. V. viii. 5. 38). The smith sought "after the man who possessed plenty of gold, with well-dried wood, with anvil (a s' m a d y u) and bellows (lit. bird's feathers) to kindle the flame" (R. V. ix. 112. 3.) Brahmanaspati is said to have "blown forth" the birth of gods, like a blacksmith (R. V. x. 72. 2). Silver is rarely mentioned (A. V. v. 28. 1), but gold very frequently. Next to gold, the word a y a s is often referred to; and since in A. V. xi. 3. 7, s' y ā m a m a y a s and l o h i t a m a y a s (black metal, red metal) are both mentioned, we may infer that smiths worked in copper too, a conclusion strengthened by the fact that copper is a holy metal even to-day and copper vessels alone are allowed to be used for holding consecrated water in all ceremonial. The metal bowls (k a m s a), of A. V. x. 10. 5 were probably of bronze. Tin (t r a p u) is also mentioned (A. V. xi. 3. 8) and lead (s ī s a m) much used in sorcery (A. V. i. 16. 2, etc). Workers in leather made casks (d h r i t i) for holding liquor (s u r ā, (R. V. i. 191. 10) or water (R. V. v. 83. 7), shields (v a r m a n) of bullock's hide (A. V. vi. 67. 3), leather-guards for the hands of the archer (h a s t a g h n ā, R. V. vi. 75. 14), drums formed of wood and bound with straps of leather (d u n d u b h i, A. V. 20. 1, R. v. i. 28. 5 etc.)

The physician (b h i s h a k) employed spells and medicaments to cure ills (A. V vi. 16). The physician was "fiend-slayer and chaser of disease" (R. V. x. 97. 6). Various diseases are named and their symptoms referred to, jaundice (h a r i t a, A.V. iv. 9 3) "white leprosy" (k i l ā s a, A. V. i. 23, 24), fever (t a k m ā) of which several varieties are mentioned, a n y e d y u, t r i t ī y a k a, u b h a y a d y u, quotidian, tertian, quartan, (A. Vi. 25. 4), continuous (s a d a n d i), summer, rainy, autumnal (A.V.v. 22.), phthisis (y a k s h m a, A. V. ii. 10. 6), cough (k ā s i k ā), herpes (p ā m ā), expectorating cough (? b a l ā s' a, A. V. iv. 9. 8), worms (k r i m i) of which numerous species are named (A. V. ii. 31, 32), rheumatism (v i s h k a n d h a A. V. i. 16. 3), scrofula (a p a c h i t, A. V. vi. 25. 1), abscess (v i d h r a d ā, A. V. vi. 127. 1), inflammation of the eyes (l o h i t a, *ib.*,) penetrating pain (v i s a l y a k a, *ib.*,) swelling of glands (plague? A. V. vi. 127. 2), anamia, (? v i l o h i t a, A. V. ix. 8. 1.), a l a j i, an eruption in the eye, dysentery (ā s r ā v a, A. V. i. 2. 4), boils (a k s h a t a, A. V. vii. 76. 4), tumours (g l a u, g a l u n t a, A. V. vi. 83. 3), palpitation (v i d h u A. V. ix. 8. 22), venereals (j ā y ā n y a, A. V. vii. 76. 3) hereditary diseases (k s h e t r i y a A. V. ii. 8, 10, etc.), heart-disease (h r i d d y o t a, A. V. i. 22. 1, h r i d ā m a y a, (A. V. v. 30. 9), debility (s e d i A. V. ii. 14. 3) convulsions (j a m b h a, A. V. ii. 4. 2), catarrh (v i k l i n d u, A. V. xii. 4. 5), elephantiasis (? s' i p a d a, R. V. vii. 50. 4). The "cold, hot and trembling" stages of malarial fever were differentiated (A. V. v. 22. 10); small-pox is probably intended by the "fever that is spotted, speckled, ruddy like a sprinkling, (A. V. v. 22. 3) and even moveable kidneys (v r i k k a u) diagnosed (A. V. vii. 96. 1).

Many other names of diseases occur but their meanings cannot be discovered, *e.g.*, s'imada (R. V. vii. 50. 4), vātīkāra (A. V. ix. 8. 20). Various drugs were used as medicines. It is noteworthy that the people of the plains knew little about these drugs; an Āsurī first discovered a black plant which was used as a remedy for (white) leprosy. (A. V. i. 24. 2). Drugs were bought from Kirāta girls who dug them upon the high ridges (s ā n u) of the mountains (A.V. x. 4. 14) and exchanged them for clothes (p a v a s t a), straw-mattresses (? d ū r s' a) and skins (a j i n a m, A. V. iv. 7. 6) and these drugs were used in the treatment of disease; many names of drugs occur in the Atharva Veda, but most of them have not yet been identified; one, p r i s' n i-p a r n i, (Hermionitis cordifolia) was used to prevent threatened abortion (A. V. ii. 25. 1) and it is interesting to note that Sus'ruta recommend the same drug for the same purpose (i. 377. 7). Besides medicines derived from plants, the earth of white ants (u p a j ī k ā) was a favourite remedy. According to K a u s' i k a sūtra 31. 26, a lump from an ant-hill was fastened on the body of a poisoned person; he was given some of it (in water) to drink; he was made to rinse his mouth with the same mixture, and was besmeared with a solution of it in warm water (Bloomfield, A t h. V e d. I n t. vi. 100.) This remedy was administered in the case of many other diseases. In the Atharva Veda it is prescribed for flux of all kinds (A. V. (ii. 3. 4), and as an antidote against poison (A. V. vi. 100). The ant is called "the daughter of the Asuras" (A. V. vi. 100. 3). The horn of the gazelle (h a r i ṇ a) was used for curing inherited (k s h e t r i y a) diseases (A. V. iii. 7. 1) and j a l ā s h a (urine) for boils, called the arrow of Rudra and the remedy was called the medicine of Rudra (r u d r a s y a b h e s h a j a m, (A. V. vi. 57. 1). Disease was regarded mostly as the result of sin against gods or possession by demons; hence the boundaries between medicine and demonology were of the flimsiest, b h e s h a j a m included both medication and exorcism. Dropsy was the fetter (p ā s′ a m) of Varuṇa; and though the association of dropsy with disease of the heart was known (A. V. vi. 24. 1), the treatment consisted in sprinkling on the patient water consecrated with the recitation of A. V. vi. 24. That water was believed to sympathetically drive out the water of dropsy. A reed was used as a catheter in cases of difficulty of micturition (A. V. i. 3. 7) but the whole of the hymn had to be recited also. In cases of fever, a frog was tied to the leg of the cot of the patient and charms were uttered to make the cool frog attract the heat of the fever (A. V. vii. 11. 6). Often the treatment was based on colour merely; red objects were placed round a patient to cure him of jaundice and Rohinī, the red goddess, was worshipped (A. V. i. 22); the "touch cure" was also resorted to, of course fortified by spells (R. V. x. 60. 12, A. V. iv. 13. 7). Aphrodisiac drugs, charms and amulets (m a ṇ i) were in great demand. Varuṇa when he became m r i t a b h r a j a, first used a s′e p h a h a r s h a ṇ ī drug and made his p a s a s d h a n u r i v a (A. V. iv. 4. 6). Since then priest-physicians sang to their patients, "a h a m t a n o m i t e p a s o a d h ī j y ā m i v a d h a n- v a n i, k r a m a s v a r s′a i v a r o h i t a m a n a v a g l ā- y a t ā s a d ā. The strength of the horse, the mule, the goat and the ram, moreover the strength of the bull bestow upon him, O controller of bodies" (A. V. iv. 4. 7, 8) and restored them to their lost virility. The s k a n d h a m a ṇ i, an amulet made from the skin on the shoulder of an elephant and tied on with hair from its tail was also employed for the same purpose (A. V. iii. 22. 6).

Though the treatment of disease was so crude, these ancient physicians had a better knowledge of anatomy than their latter-day descendants because they cut many animals for sacrifice and had to do it skilfully without displeasing the gods by mangling the limbs of the animal, (R. V. i. 162. 20, A V. ix. v. 4.) and "skilful slaughterers loosed the joints of animals" (A. V. ix. 3. 3) carefully. Besides the obvious parts of the body, the following out-of-the-way ones were named. Vertebræ, kīkasā (A. V. ii. 33. 2). ankle-joint, gulpha (A. V. x. 2. 1), collar-bone, kaphoḍa, (A V. x. 2. 4), hind-head, kakaṭikā (A. V. x. 2. 8.) entrails, vakshaṇā (A. V. ii. 5. 5.), bladder, vasti (A. V. i. 3. 8), ureters, gavīnī (A. V. i. 3. 6), perineum, vijrāmā (A. V. vii. 76. 2), rectum, vanisṭhu (A. V. ix. 7. 12). As examples of poetical names we have patívedana, husband-finder, for the breasts (A. V. viii. 6. 1), a bowl (chamasa) with orifice sideways, bottom-side up, for the skull (A. V. x. 8. 9). The difference between arterial and venous blood is referred to (aruṇā, lohinī, A. V. x. 2. 11) and hirā and dhamanī used in the sense of veins and arteries (A. V. i. 17. 3). The surgeons used ligatures (abhis'riṭ) for stopping bleeding (R. V. viii. 1. 12) and "built a rampart of sand," *i.e.*, probably filled bandages with wet sand for the same purpose (A. V. i. 17. 4). The surgeon, like the physician, used both knives and mantras. (A. V. i. 17).

The Brāhmaṇa purohitas, priests of kings, nobles and common people, abounded in the land (R. V. x. 103. 7). Teachers of hymns taught boys to learn them by rote (R. V. x. 103. 5). Rishis composed hymns and received as rewards wreaths of flower or gold, asses, fleecy sheep (R. V. vāl. viii. 3), oxen, bamboos, logs, well-tanned skins, tufts of balbaja grass for making mats, mares (*Ib.* vii. 2. 3) slave girls, kine (R. V. viii. 19 36, 37), chariots with mares and steeds decked with pearls (R. V. vii. 18. 22, 23) and houses (A. V. ix. 3). The other professions mentioned are those of the dancer (n r i t ū), male (R. V. i. 130. 7) and female (R. V. i. 92. 4), the spy (s p a s' a, R. V. vii. 87. 3), the barber (v a p t ā, R. V. x. 142. 4) who wetted the beard with hot water before shaving it (A. V. vi. 68. 1), the vintner (s u r ā v a t a) (R. V. i. 191. 10), the currier (c h a r - m a m n a) (R. V. viii. 5. 38), the usurer (R. V. viii. 55. 10), the tamer of elephants (A. V. iii. 22), the horse-groom (R. V. viii. 55. 3), the soothsayer (a d d h ā t i, A. V. vi. 76, 2) the weather prophet (s' a k a d h ū m a, lit. dung-smoker, A. V. vi. 128. 1), the fisher (p a u ñ j i s h ṭ h a A. V. x. 4. 19), the potter, (k u l ā l a, A. V. iv. 17. 4), the spell-fashioner, *i.e.*, the maker of images for sorcery (k r i t y a - k r i t), the digger of roots (mūlī, A. V. v. 31. 12); the s' u k l a y a j u s s a m h i t ā names these other professions, makers of arrows, bows, bowstrings (i s h u k ā r a, d h a n u s h k ā r a, j y ā k ā r a), the rope-maker (r a j j u s- a r j a), the hunter (m ṛ i g a y u), thefemale cane-splitter (b i d a l a k ā r ī), the female worker in thorns (k a ṇ ṭ a k ī- k ā r ī), the embroideress (p e s' a s k ā r ī), the seller of love-charms (s m a r a k ā r ī), the wood-bringer (d ā r v ā h ā r a), the washer-woman (v ā s a h p a l p ū l ī), the female dyer (r a j- a y i t r ī), the female ointment-maker (a ñ j a n ī k ā r ī), the female scabbard-maker (k o s' a k ā r ī), the hide-dresser (a j i- n e s a n d h a), the panegyrist (m ā g a d h a). (S. Y. S. xxx).

The profession of war was carried on by the fighting classes; but Rishis and Brāhmaṇas followed the army to the battlefield and took part in the fight (R. V. vii. 33. 1), Indra was the war-god, who, propitiated by liberal offerings of soma juice and the fat of buffaloes and oxen, led his worshippers on to victory (R. V. x. 160. 3, vi. 31. 5, etc.)

Some wars were raiding expeditions for the capture of cattle (g a v i s h ṭ i, A. V. iv. 24. 5, R. V. vā.l. v. 8, v. 6. 7) or expeditions to recover cattle stolen and punish the raiders (R. V. vi. 22. 3, ii. 12. 3) or for capturing women (R. V. ix. 67, 10—12). "Two opposing hosts contend in battle for seed and offspring, waters, kine or corn-lands" (R. V. vi. 25. 4.), "for wives" (R. V. iv. 17. 16). "Men in fury rush together for running streams, for pastures and for houses" (R. V. vii. 56. 22). Others, like the war of the ten kings (R. V. vii. 84. 7) were fought between leagued bands of Aryas and Dāsas on the one hand and other similar bands on the other. Warriors marched to battle with raised banners (R. V. x. 103. 1). Many flags were used; the meeting of heaven and earth is compared to the meeting of "flag with flag in battle" (R. V. i. 103. 1). The war-drum was beaten as a signal of the beginning of the fight and the heroes grasping weapons specially burnished (R. V. i. 92. 1) and uttering "far-resounding shouts" (R. V. v. 54. 12) rushed to the fray, "impetuous, bursting forward, like flames of fire in form, exulting, with pointed arrows" (R. V. x. 84. 1). Charioteers "urged the chargers to their (utmost) speed on the uneven road and on a toilsome path, like falcons, eager for renown, speeding like rivers rushing down a deep descent, responsive to the urging call, that come like birds attracted to the bait, held in by reins in both the driver's hands" (R. V. vi. 46. 13. 14). The heroes rushed on shouting (R. V. i. 87. 5), decked with glittering ornaments, lances on their shoulders (R. V. i. 64. 4), dagger and quoit in hand (R. V. i. 168. 3) and decked with "anklets on feet, gold chains on breasts" (R. V. v. 54. 11), bracelets on their upper arms (these jewels corresponded to the medals of the modern times and were given to successful warriors by royal patrons) (R V. i. 64. 10.)

They wore "well-sewn armour" (R. V. i. 31. 15) and looked "self-luminous, with ornaments and spears, with golden wreaths and anklets, arrayed on chariots and with bows" (R. V. v. 53. 4). "The warrior's look is like a thunderous rain-cloud's, when, armed with mail, he seeks the lap of battle. With bow let us win kine, with bow the battle, with bow the victors in our hot encounters. The bow brings grief and sorrow to the foeman: armed with the bow may we subdue all regions. Close to his ear as fain to speak, she presses, holding her well-loved in her embraces. Strained on the bow, she whispers like a woman, this bowstring that preserves us in the combat. These, meeting like a woman and her lover, bear, mother-like, their child upon their bosom. May the two bow-ends, starting swift asunder, scatter, in unison, the foes that hate us. With many a son, father of many daughters, he [the quiver] clangs and clashes as he goes to battle; slung on the back, pouring his brood, the quiver vanquishes all opposing bands and armies. Upstanding in the car, the skilful charioteer guides his strong horses on, whithersoever he will. See and admire the strength of those controlling reins which from behind declare the will of him who drives. Horses whose hoofs rain dust are neighing loudly, yoked to the chariots, showing forth their vigour. With their forefeet descending on the foeman, they, never flinching, trample and destroy them ......He [the whip, k a s'a], who urgest horses, drives sagacious horses to the fray. It [the leather-guard on the archer's left arm] compasses the arm with serpent's windings, fending away the friction of the bow-strings: so may the guard, well-skilled in all its duties, guard manfully the man from every quarter. Now to the shaft with venom smeared, tipped with deer-horn, with iron mouth, celestial, of Parjanya's seed [*i.e.*, made of reeds that grow in the rains], be this great adoration paid. Loosed from the bow-string fly away, thou arrow, sharpened by our prayer. Go to the foemen, strike them home, and let no one be left alive" (R. V. vi. 75. 1—7, 13—16). Probably elephants were also used in war. One very obscure passage as interpreted by Sāyaṇa refers to "two mad elephants bending their heads and smiting the foe" (R. V. x. 106 6). Thus the four "limbs of war," gaja ratha turaga padāti existed in the age of the Mantras. The war-drum (dundubhī), sounded both to indicate the starting of the fight (R. V. vi. 47. 31) and the success of the winning side (R. V. i. 28. 5), is frequently eulogized in the hymns. "Send forth thy voice aloud through earth and heaven, and let the world in all its breadth regard thee; O drum, accordant with the Gods and Indra, drive thou afar, yea, very far, our foemen. Thunder out strength and fill us full of vigour: yea, thunder forth and drive away all dangers. Drive hence, O war-drum, drive away misfortune: thou art the fist of Indra: show thy firmness" (R. V. vi. 47. 29, 30). "Found suddenly like a bull in a herd, do thou, seeking kine, bellow at [them], winning booty; pierce thou with pain the heart of our adversaries; let our foes leaving their villages, go urged forth [by thee]" (A. V. v. 20. 3). The drums were covered with the leather of cows (A. V. v. 21. 3) or of antelopes (*Ib.* 7). Besides the weapons enumerated above, spiked clubs, prototypes of the sacred sacrificial post (yūpa), clubs of iron (ghana, R. V. i. 36. 16, matya, A. V. xi. 2. 19), nets stretched on poles, for trapping the enemy (A. V. viii. 8. 5), missiles (senya, A. V. i. 20. 2, heti, A. V. i. 26. 1., sāyaka, A. V. iv. 31. 6), "flying like lightning from the strong man's arms" (R. V.

vii, 25. 1), the chief of which were iron missiles shot from slings of leather (R. V. i. 121. 9), sharp stone missiles similarly shot (R. V. vi. 6. 5) and "darts of stone burning with fiery flame" (R. V. vii. 104. 5), and knives attached to fellies of chariots (R. V. i. 166. 10) were also used. The war-chariot is praised equally with the war-drum. "Lord of the wood, be firm and strong in body; be, bearing us, a brave victorious hero. Show forth thy strength, compact with straps of leather, and let thy rider win all spoils of battle." (R. V. vi. 47. 26). The body of the warrior was protected by mailed armour (v a r m a, R. V. vi. 75. 18, k a v a c h a, V. S. xvi. 1.), and the head by a helmet (b i l m a, V. S. xvi. 1); he also protected himself with a shield (v a r ū t h a, A. V. v. 5. 4). The bow was made of a shaft and a string (v ī ḍ u, A. V. i. 2. 2.) of cow-gut, as the Atharva Veda poetically describes it, "the kine embracing the tree make the quivering dextrous reed sing" (i. 2. 3). The arrow (i s h u) was composed of the reed body (s' a r a, A. V. iv. 7. 4), the barb (a p ā s h ṭ h a, A. V. iv. 6. 5.) and the tip (s' a l y a, *Ib.* 4). Some unidentifiable weapons (v a d h a, A. V. vi. 13. 1) are also mentioned, *e.g.*, a r b u d i, n y a r b u d i, t r i s h a n d h i (A. V. xi. 10). The last was probably the same as t r i s ū l a. At the end of a battle, the punishments awarded to the defeated enemies were very cruel. Indra defeated Vritra and turned him into a castrate (v a d h r i, R. V. i. 32. 7), and his worshippers prayed to him "emasculate (n i r a k s h ṇ u h i) his [*i.e.*, the king's] enemies" (A, V. iv. 22. 1). So in battles when they had the chance, they split the m u s h k a u and cut off the s' e p a s (A. V. iv. 37. 7) of their foes. Piercing the vitals (A. V. v. 8. 9), hewing off arms (A. V. vi. 65. 2), stripping off the skin, cutting the flesh in pieces wrenching off sinews, breaking the bones, and smiting out the marrow, were other forms of dealing with the foe, which when they could not be done actually on the battle-field were attempted to be effected by witch-craft (A. V. xii. 5. 68. 70). The bodies of the slain were, after the battle, thrown into a pit. "The foes were slaughtered and in the pit of death (vailasthānam) lay pierced and mangled" (R. V. i. 133. 1). The victors then presented the gods with their "share of glory" (R. V. i. 73. 5). Images drawn from war abound in the Mantras. "Sheltering arms surround a man like the two ends of a bow strained with cord" (A. V. i. 1. 3). "Lightning is the arrow of the gods" (A. V. i. 13. 4). "The bowstring sings triumph to the swift and whizzing arrows" (A. V. i. 2. 3). "The broad-chested speckled deer stand like a king's armies on the field of battle" (R. V. i. 170. 6). "The fastened frame of the war-drum hath roared as it were a lion, like a bull bellowing" (A. V. v. 20. 1).

It has already been proved that the people of India traded with foreign countries in the age preceding that with which we are dealing now. In the Mantras we find references to "those who desiring wealth send ships to the sea" (R. V. i. 48. 3), to voyages of "parties of merchants going on the ocean (R. V. i. 56. 2) in ships with a hundred oars (R. V. i. 116. 5), "to distant lands for sale and barter." (A. V. iii. 15. 4). The merchant, before he started on his journey "seeking riches with riches" (A. V. iii. 15. 6) sang a hymn to the "Merchant Indra," who traffics with his worshippers, receiving oblation in exchange for his help (A. V. iii. 15. 1). Indra tells his worshipper in S. Y. S. iii. 50, "Give me, I give thee gifts: bestow upon me, and I bestow on thee," and the latter replies, "To me present thy merchandise, and I to thee will give my wares." The merchant offered fuel and ghi and other fire-oblations and sang hymns to help him to gain success in his business and earn a "hundred treasures" (R. V. iii. 18. 3) and went to far-off lands for "interchange of merchandise" (A. V. iii. 15. 4). Agni watched over the merchant's children, his body, his kine, his life (A. V. iii. 15. 7) and he offered a portion of his profits to the God. "Still to thee ever, will we bring oblation, as to a stabled horse, O Jātavedas; joying in food and in the growth of riches may we thy servants, Agni, never suffer." (A. V. iii. 15. 8). The return of the merchant to his house after a long absence is the subject of a touching hymn in the Atharva Veda. "I, prudent, bringing power, a treasure winner, with amicable eye that strikes no terror, come, praising and kind-thoughted, to these houses: be not afraid of me, be glad and joyful. Let these delightful houses that are rich in power and store of milk, replete with wealth and standing firm, become aware of our approach. These houses we invoke whereon the distant exile set his thought, wherein dwells many a friendly heart; let them be ware of our approach. Thus greeted, ye of ample wealth, friends who enjoy delightful sweets, be ever free from hunger, free from thirst! Ye, houses, fear us not. Kind greeting to the cattle here, kind greeting to the goats and sheep! Then of the food within our homes, kind greeting to the pleasant drink. Full of refreshment, full of charms, of laughter and felicity, be ever free from hunger, free from thirst; ye houses, fear us not." (vii. 60. 1. 6). The Rig Veda mantras have preserved the name of a great merchant of ancient days, Bṛibu, who set himself over the highest head of the merchants, "like the wide bush on Gangā's bank" (R. V. vi. 45. 31) and whose good bounty, "swift as the rushing wind," led him to give a thousand liberal gifts to the Rishis (R. V. vi. 45. 32, 33). The ordinary merchant was not so bountiful as Bṛibu and hence the word P a ṇ i, trader, is frequently used in the sense of niggard (R. V. vi. 51. 14, vii. 22. 6). Pieces of gold (r u k m ā, A. V. ix 5. 14) and lumps of gold (R V. vi. 47. 23) were used in place of coins; besides in R. V. viii. 67. 2, there is a reference to the golden Manā, an old Semitic measure or coin. The merchants that traded with the Semitic countries brought from Mesopotamia or beyond, the North Semitic alphabet about 1000 B.C. The Brāhmaṇas soon elaborated it to suit the Indian phonetic system and wrote books in this Brāhmī alphabet. The very late Mantras in A. V. xix. 68. and 72. distinctly refer to taking the book (the Veda) out of a box at the beginning of studies and putting it back into it at the end of it. "Both of the broad and the narrow, I with power unclose the mouth. With these when we have taken up the Veda we pay the holy rites." "Within the chest wherefrom we before took out the Veda, this do we now deposit. Wrought is the sacrifice by the power of Brahma. Through this fervour assist me here, ye gods." The former mantra was used, according to Kaus'ika Sutra during the u p a n a y a n a m, at the beginning of studies (139. 10.) and the latter, during the s n ā t a k a rite, at the end of studies (139. 25.) The "Veda" in these passages has been interpreted by some as the broom made of a bunch of grass; but it is absurd to imagine that the broom, of all things, would be deposited in a chest and taken out when wanted.

Caste, as we know it now in India, a theoretical framework of four classes, each class sub-divided into an unlimited number of sections, the members of each of which are not allowed to marry members of others, did not exist in ancient

India. But the three higher castes are frequently mentioned, and the Sudra, more than half-a-dozen times, in the Mantras. The phrase "Arya and Sudra," occurs a few times (A. V. iv. 20. 4, etc.) and evidently means, as in modern days, one who is (theoretically) qualified for the fire-cult and who is not. In the age of the Mantras the priests were generally Brāhmaṇas and though Rājanyas like Vis'vāmitra (R. V. iii. 53. 9) and Devāpi (R. V. x. 98) acted as priests, this was exceptional and Brāhmaṇas were generally purohitas (R. V. iv. 50. 9, x. 71. 8, x. 85. 16, etc.) The four "castes" are referred to in R. V. x. 90. 12 and i. 113. 6. Though the people were divided into "castes" there was no restriction with regard to marriage. "When a woman has had ten former husbands, not Brāhmaṇas, if a Brāhmaṇa 'takes her hand,' it is he alone who is her husband" (A. V. v. 17. 8). Brāhmaṇa women were not regarded as sacrosanct but could be restored to their husbands after being seduced (R. V. x. 109. 6). Curses are levelled against people who "shut up" within their houses a Brāhmaṇa's wife (A. V. v. 17. 12. 18), thereby proving that this was not uncommon. Professions, too, were not restricted to particular castes. Says a mantra, referring to the diversity of men's tastes, "I am a poet, my father is a doctor, my mother a grinder of corn. With our different views, seeking after gain, we run, as after cattle." (R. V. ix. 112. 3). A Brāhmaṇa physician is also referred to in R. V. x. 97. 6, 22. During the age of the Mantras, the influence of the Brāhmaṇas steadily increased and their claims to social predominance insistently urged. "In his own house he dwells in peace and comfort, to him for ever holy food flows richly, to him the people with free will pay homage—the king with whom the Brāhmaṇa has precedence. He, unopposed, is master of the riches of his own subjects and of hostile people. The Gods uphold the king with their protection who helps the Brāhmaṇa when he seeks his favour" (R. V. iv. 50. 8, 9). The Brāhmaṇas claimed to be human gods (A. V. iii. 32, vi. 13. 1) and those that reviled them would be punished by the gods on high. "May he, though bathed in sweat, form empty wishes, who blames the sacred rite of him, who toils to serve you" [Maruts] (R. V. v. 42. 10). The Brāhmaṇa could punish those that regarded him not, because then "his tongue becomes a bowstring, his voice an [arrow] neck, his teeth shafts (n ā ḍ ī k ā) smeared with penance [for poison]" (A. V. v. 18 8). The Brāhmaṇas hurled their arrows (*i.e.*, spells) in volleys (s' a r a v y ā) (*Ib.* 9). They were experts in witchcraft (a b h i c h ā r a) and hence their property was to be respected. A Brāhmaṇa's cow should not be eaten by a non-Brāhmaṇa, for fear that terrible consequences would flow from the sin (A. V. v. 18. 1, 4, 10—11). Those who spat upon a Brāhmaṇa, or who shot mucus at him, would sit in the midst of a stream of blood, devouring hair. (A. V. v. 19. 3). Demands for priestly fees (d a k s h i n ā), exaggerated accounts of royal liberality to Brāhmaṇas in the d ā n a s t u t i hymns (*vide* R. V. v ā l. 7. 8, x. 107, etc.), peremptory injunctions like, "distribute treasure to the Brāhmaṇas" (R. V. x. 85. 29) occur constantly in the Mantras. Besides heavy fees, minor perquisites, were not despised by the Brāhmaṇas. The cow that gave birth to twin-calves had to be made over to a Brāhmaṇa (A. V. iii. 28. 2); so, too, a sterile cow (v a s' ā, A. V. xii. 4). While thus hankering for wealth, the Brāhmaṇas recognized the necessity for deserving the respect of their patrons. The idle Brāhmaṇa was condemned. "When friendly Brāhmaṇas sacrifice together with mental impulse which the heart hath fashioned, they leave one far behind through their attainments and some who count as Brāhmaṇas wander elsewhere. Those men who step not back and move not forward, nor Brāhmanas nor preparers of libations, having attained to *vāk* in sinful fashion spin out their thread in ignorance like spinsters" (R. V. x. 71. 8, 9). "Better the speaking than the silent Brāhmana" (R. V. x. 117. 7). The Brāhmana while claiming his privileges was fully conscious of the obligations of social eminence, of *noblesse oblige*. He had a high ideal of intellectual attainments; he craved for attaining the power of speaking "brilliant words among the people" (A. V. vi. 69. 2); he strove to attain "the wisdom (*medhā*) that the Ribhus know, the wisdom that the Asuras know, the excellent wisdom that the seers know" (A. V. vi. 109. 3). He prayed for keenness of perception (*ākūti*), for high thoughts (*chittam*), for the desire (*kāma*) that stimulates intellectual greatness (A. V. xix. 4. 2, 4), for the increase of wisdom (A. V. xix. 41), for the unbroken continuance in him of that knowledge and power (*brahmā*) which would enable him always to remain an ideal Brāhmaṇa (A. V. xix. 42). He desired to be able to constantly sing songs in the praise of the gods, hymns "that go forth like torrents, as rivers eddying under banks, flow seaward" (R. V. i. 190. 7) and required the community to keep him in affluence in return for his service. There was a difference between the Rishi and the mere priest. The Rishis composed hymns and elaborated various forms of the fire-rite. The priests of whom various classes are mentioned (R. V. ii. 1, 2, etc.) had definite functions in the rites. The Rishi was the inspired seer and came from various classes of society (and both sexes) and his authority was due to his poetic inspiration, his knowledge of the secret names of the gods by which alone they could be coerced (R. V. x. 45. 2, x. 55. 1) and his insight into the methods by which the gods could be flattered into doing what their worshippers wanted. The priest came from the priestly classes and was an important factor of society. Without him fire-rites could not be performed. The profession of the Brāhmaṇa was quite as well recognized as any other profession. "The carpenter seeks something broken, the doctor a patient, the Brāhmaṇa some one to offer oblations" (R. V. ix. 112. 1). The word brahmā, besides indicating a man of the priestly caste, had also the specific signification of a head priest in a yajña. "Thine, Agni, is the office of hotā, thine the function of potā, thine the duty of neshṭā, thou art the agnidh of the sacrificer; thine is the office of the pras′āstā, thou dost the work of the adhvaryu, thou art the brahmā and the lord of the house in our dwellings" (R. V. ii. 1. 2). Some Rājanyas were Rishis and hence acted as priests as when Devāpi celebrated a rite to secure rainfall, but there is no trace in the mantras of priest-kings, like the patesi of the ancient Babylonians.

The people lived in wooden houses (s′ālā A. V. iii. 12. 1). Brahmaṇaspati fashioned the Earth and Heaven from wood (R. V. x. 31. 7) as carpenters fashioned wooden houses. Wood was used largely because the Indians had in very early days attained great proficiency in wood-work and wood was very easily procured. Even the Punjab was in those days well-wooded and the destruction of forests, which has since turned the valley of the Indus into an arid desert by not intercepting wind-borne moisture, had not gone far. Hence wood-architecture was highly popular. The houses were firmly fixed in the ground with wooden pegs (R. V. vii. 99. 3) and rested on wooden pillars (s t h ū ṇ ā R. V. i 59 1). Besides the corner-posts, two to ten side-posts strong "like elephant's feet" (A. V. ix. 3. 17), were used for constructing houses (A. V. ix. 3. 21). The beams (v a m s' a, A. V. iii. 12. 6, because they were of bamboo), used to support the roof, were tied together by strong cords. The beams and roof were supported by props (u p a m i t, p r a t i m i t), and cross-beams (p a r i m i t A.V. ix. 3. 1); they were held together by bolts (n a h a n a), ropes (p r ā n ā h a), clamps (s a n d a m s' a), dovetails (p a l a d a) and reeds (p a r i s v a ñ j a l y a, (A.V. ix.3.4,5). The roof consisted of the thousand-eyed net (a k s h u), wicker-work mats (i ṭ a) stretched out on the division-line (v i s h ū v a t i), like the net-like dressing of the hair of ladies (*Ib*. 8) and "a robe of grass" (c h a d i s, A. V. iii 7. 3), "to ward off the fierce heat" (R. V. iv. 44. 7). The houses, being mostly constructed of wood were moveable. "Like a woman (v a d h ū), O dwelling, we carry thee where we will" (A. V. ix. 3. 24). Such houses were constructed and presented to Brāhmaṇas who took out their various parts with the recitation of the mantras of A. V. ix. 3 and refixed them with mantras on their own sites. The houses of the rich had "four walls" (A. V. iii. 7. 3), and the poor lived as now in circular huts of wattle daubed with clay and "clad with straw" (A. V. iii. 12, 5). The better houses had a store-room (h a v i r d h ā n a m), a ladies' bower, a men's general living room and an Agni's hall (a g n i s' ā l a m, A. V. ix. 3. 7), and the very rich owned, besides, a treasure-room paved with rock (a d r i b u d h n a h a y a m n i d h i ḥ, (R. V. x. 108. 7). In royal houses the harem was called m ā h i s h a, as we learn from Kaus. Sūt. 17. 6. Attached to the houses was a courtyard (p r o s h ṭ h a m R. V. vii. 55. 8) and the compounds were fenced round with sticks (p a r i d h i, R. V. i. 59. 6). The floor was covered with reed mats (u p a s t a r a ṇ a m A. V. v. 19. 12), on which were placed cushions (ā s t a r a ṇ a m, A. V. xv. 3. 7) and poorer people spread grass on the floor. The spreading of a seat of grass for guests was an ancient custom and hence gods invoked at a sacrifice were seated on grass (R. V. ix. 59. 3). The rich slept on beds (t a l p a m) spread on benches (p r o s h ṭ h a m) or cots (va hyam, A.V. iv. 5. 3) made of a framework of wood tied with strings or tapes and provided with bolsters, coverlets and blankets (u p a d h ā n a m, A.V. xiv. 2. 65, u p a b a r h a ṇ a m, A. V. xv. 3. 7, u p a r i s' ạ y a n a m, A. V. ix. 6. 9). Besides benches and cots, the household furniture consisted of chairs (ā s a n d ī, A. V. xiv. 2. 65), boxes (k o s' a m, R. V. x. 42. 2, A. V. i. 14. 4) leather-bags (k r i v i, R. V. v. 44. 4) and domestic utenils, such as curd-skins (d h r i t i, R. V. vi. 48. 18) bowls (d h i s h a n a, R. V. vi. 8. 13), some of which were decorated with carvings (A. V. xix. 49. 8), buckets with hoops (ā b a n d h r a, A. V. iv. 16. 7), vessels of various materials, ranging from silver (A. V. viii. 10. 23)down to gourd (*Ib.*29), metal vessels in nests (A. V.ix. 3. 20), sieves (s'ū r p a m, A. V. ix. 6. 16), wooden spoons, stirring-sticks, spits (s r u k, d a r v ī, n e k s h a ṇ a m, A. V. ix.6.17), pots of various kinds, (ā ya v a n a m, d r o ṇ a k a l a- s a m, k u m b h a m), mortars and pestles (u l ū k h a l a m, m u s a l a m, A. V. x 9. 26), bellows (t i t a u, R.V. x. 72. 2) pressing or grinding stones (a d h i s h a v a ṇ a u, broad d v ā- v i v a j a g h a n a u, R. V. i. 28. 2), the s' i k y a, a hanging bracket of ropes, (A. V. ix. 3. 6), etc. The valuables in the house were secured in a box before the people retired for the night; they then repeated the following prayers to the night. "O night, the earthly space hath been filled with the father's orderings; great, thou spreadest thyself to the seats of the sky; bright darkness comes on. She, of whom the further limit is not seen, nor what separates; in her, everything that stirs goes to rest; uninjured may we, O wide darksome night, attain thy further limit; may we O excellent one, attain thy further limit. The men-watching lookers (stars) that are thine, O night, ninety-nine, eighty-eight are they, also seventy-seven of thine; and sixty-six, O wealthy one, fifty-five, O pleasant one, four and forty, three and thirty, O mighty one; and two of thine and twenty of thine, O night; eleven the least, with those protectors to-day do thou protect us, daughter of the sky. Let no demon, mischief-plotter, master us; let no thief to-day master our kine, nor wolf our sheep; nor a robber our horses, O excellent one; nor the sorceresses our men. Do thou, O night, make the snake blind, breathless (?) headless; grind up the two jaws of the wolf; cast the thief into the snare. With thee, O night, we stay; we shall sleep; do thou watch; yield refuge to our kine, horses, men." (A. V. xix. 47). "Now then what things we note, or what things are within the box, those things we commit to thee. O night! mother! commit thou us to the dawn; let the dawn commit us to the day, the day to thee, O shining one. Whatsoever flies here, whatsoever that is crawling is here, whatsoever creature is on the mountain, from that do thou, O night, protect us. Do thou protect behind, thou in front, thou from above and from below; do thou guard us, O shining one; here we are, thy praisers. They who follow the night, and who watch over beings, who defend all cattle, they watch over ourselves, they watch over our cattle. Verily I know thy name, O night; thou art ghī-dropping by name; as such Bharadvāja knows thee; do thou watch over our property" (A. V. xix. 48).

The people ate both animal and vegetable food, Horses (A. V. vi. 71. 1), bulls (R. V. i. 164. 43) buffaloes

(R. V. v. 29. 7), rams (R. V. x. 27. 17) and goats (R. V. i. 162. 3) were killed on slaughter-benches (s ū n ā, R. V. x. 86. 18), cooked in caldrons (R. V. iii. 53. 22) and eaten. The eating of fishes and birds must have also prevailed because fishing and bird-catching are referred to (A. V. vii. 117. 1, x. 4. 19). Of animal food derived from the living animal, milk (R. V. x 49. 10), sometimes mixed with honey (R. V. viii 4. 8) brought by "toiling bees" (R. V. x. 106. 9), ghī (R. V. iv. 58) butter (s a r p i s, A. V. ix. 6. 41), and curds (R. V. vi. 57. 2) were consumed. Y a v a is frequently mentioned in the sense of corn in general or barley. Rice, barley, beans and sesamum were the chief vegetable food-stuffs of the day (A. V. vi. 140. 4). Grain was eaten parched (d h ā n ā, R. V. iii. 35. 3) or made into cakes (a p ū p a m, R. V. iii. 52. 7, p u r o ḍ ā s' a m, A. V. xii. 4. 35) or boiled in water (o d a n a m, A. V. iii. 34, 35) or in milk (R. V. viii. 66. 10). Meal boiled with curd into k a r a m b h a (A. V. iv. 7. 2) and gruel, *i.e.*, parched meal boiled in milk (m a n t h a, A. V. x. 6. 2) were other forms of food. The boiling of rice in pots is poetically described in A. V .xii. 3. 29. "Heated, they rage, they dance on, they cast about their foam in countless bubbles, like a woman that is in her season what time ye waters and the rice-grains mingle." As now, hot freshly cooked food was preferred to cold food (R. V. x. 79. 3). Fruits were also eaten (R. V. i. 90. 8). Food was served on leaf platters, the lotus-leaf being commonly used for the purpose (A. V. viii. 10. 27). Skins filled with honey (R. V. iv. 45. 3, 4), or curds (R. V. vi. 49. 18), jars of honey, (R. V. i. 117. 6), rice husked by slave-girls (A. V. xii. 3. 13), and stored in earthen vessels (A. V. vi. 142. 1), and flour obtained by grinding corn in mill-stones (d r i s h a t, A. V. ii. 31. 1), were stocked in houses. Other edibles referred to are various parts of the lotus plant called bisa, s'ālūka s'aphaka, mulālī (A. V. iv. 34. 5), urvara (gourd A. V. vi. 14. 2), and the sugar-cane (A. V. i. 34. 5). The chief drinks of the people were soma and surā. The soma plant was made into a paste between two stones, strained through a woollen cloth (R. V. viii. 2. 2), mixed with fresh or curdled milk (R. V. viii. 2. 9) and drunk. Sometimes it was mixed with meal and cooked with milk and eaten (R. V. ix. 46. 4). Bhang is used in these ways in modern India. Soma is described as the "sweet juice that makes us eloquent" (R. V. viii. 1. 25). "When drunk they [the soma-draughts] contend in thy stomach, as men maddened with liquor" (R. V. viii. 2. 12). Surā was distilled from barley or rice and was stored in jars (R. V. i. 116. 7) or in skins (R. V. i. 191. 10); it was sometimes mixed with milk when drunk. (A. V. ii. 26. 5). A sweet drink called kīlālam is mentioned (A. V. iv. 11. 10); there was besides madhu, referred to frequently but in some places of uncertain meaning.

Chariots and carts drawn by oxen (A. V. iii. 11. 5), mules (A. V. viii. 8. 22) or horses were the chief means of transport. It has already been pointed out that the chariots were not primitive ones; numerous names of various parts of the chariot occur frequently in the hymns, *e.g.*, pavi, tyre of the wheel (R. V. i. 180. 1), skambhāsa, pillars supporting the top (R. V. i. 34. 2), vandhuram, the seat of the charioteer (R. V. i. 5. 28), also, the frame-work of the carriage (R. V. viii. 47. 2), rabhī, shaft, īshā, pole, aksha, axle (R. V. viii. 5. 29), pratidhi, cross-piece (A. V. xiv. 1. 8), sphya, splints (A. V. xi. 3. 9). Besides well-made cars, there were rough carts (vipatha, A. V. xv. 2. 6), some of which, at least, had primitive stone wheels. But naturally, the chariots of the nobles drawn by horses are most frequently described. "Bound by the neck and by the flanks and by the mouth, the vigorous courser speedeth after the whip and drawing himself together springs along the winding roads" (R. V. iv. 40. 4). Car-oxen were emasculated (m u s h-k a b a r h a, A. V. iii. 9. 2). "Roads for people to go upon and tracks (v a r t m ā for car and cart" were made (A. V. xii. 1. 47); some roads must have been very bad for sorrows are bidden to pass away as car-drivers avoid bad roads (R. V. viii. 47. 5). Before starting on a journey in cars, a blessing was invoked. "Strong be the pair of oxen, firm the axles, let not the pole slip nor the yoke be broken. May Indra keep the yoke-pins from decaying: attend us, thou whose fellies are uninjured. O Indra, give our bodies strength, strength to the bulls who draw the wains. Enclose thee [axle] in the heart of khadira-wood, in the car wrought of s'ims'apā firm. Show thyself strong, O axle, fixed and strengthened: throw us not from the car whereon we travel. Let not this sovereign of the wood leave us forlorn or injure us. Safe may we be until we reach our homes and rest us and unyoke." (R. V. iii. 53 17. 20). "Trees for shelter," no doubt by the sides of roads are mentioned in R. V. vii. 95. 5, chief among them being the As'vattha and the Nyagrodha (A. V. iv. 37. 4), also fair paths with pleasant grass (R. V. i. 90. 6) "where flowing d ū r v ā ponds, where fountains spring or a pond rich in lotuses" (A. V. vi. 106. 1). The Rishis frequently prayed to the gods to lead them on to "broad paths for travel" (R. V. vii. 35. 15) and "straight, thornless roads" (R. V. x. 85. 23). The cars were generally two-wheeled (R. V. x. 85. 11). Ordinarily two horses were yoked to a chariot and sometimes four (R. V. i. 126. 4);

it was considered disreputable for a rich man to drive in a one-horse car. "Men come not with one horse to sacred sessions; thus they obtain no honour in assemblies" (A. V. xx. 125. 3). Well-trained horses (v ā h a, A. V. vi. 102. 1) were harnessed to the chariots; the king-horse was called r ā j ā s' v a and the side-horse, p r a s h ṭ i (A. V. xiii. 1. 21, vi. 102. 2). The various parts of the harness of horses are named, *e.g.*, k a k s h y a, girth (R. V. i. 10. 8) r a s' m i, bridle, a b h ī s' a v a, reins (R. V. iv. 36. 1.). References to riding are not so frequent as to chariot-driving. Riders are called s ā d i n a h, those with seats in A. V. xi. 10. 24. "A horseman's day-journey" is said to be "three y o j a n a m, five y o j a n a m'," (A. V. vi. 131. 3). The altar of the As'vins is thus described. "Like a strong horse with a fair back it standeth, whereon, as in a lap, ye seat you firmly" (R. V. vii. 70. 1). The Maruts, among the gods, were great riders. "O heroes, lordliest of all, who are ye that have singly come forth from a region most remote? Where are your horses, where the reins? How came ye? How had ye the power? The whip is laid upon the flank. The heroes stretch their thighs apart, like women when the babe is born." (R. V. v. 61. 1—3). Men rode on horses with "tails like peacock's plumes" (R. V. iii. 45. 1) to cattle-raiding expeditions, raising much dust (A. V. iv. 21. 4) as well as to battle (R. V. vi. 24. 6). Horses were well-tended; they were "cleaned" (R. V. iv. 15. 6) and "bathed" (R. V. viii. 22. 2). Sacrifice is compared to a chariot in A. V. x. 107. 7 and innumerable similes from the car are found in the mantras. Horses, too, provide the Vedic poets with similes, *e.g.*, "who knows to distinguish sense and folly of men, like straight and crooked backs of horses" (R. V. iv. 2. 11). "Lead us on to pleasant ways as men lead horses to an easy ford" (R. V. viii. 47. 11).

Boats and ships are frequently mentioned in the hymns; but the authors were apparently unacquainted with the mouth of the Indus river nor had they much knowledge of the sea. Therefore the one shipwreck frequently referred to, that of Bhujyu, must have been a matter of hearsay knowledge gathered from travellers. The more important passages dealing with this shipwreck and the rescue of Bhujyu run as follows:—"As a dead man leaves his riches, Tugra left Bhujyu in the cloud of waters. Ye [As'vins] brought him back in animated vessels, traversing air, unwetted by billows. Bhujyu ye bore with winged things, Nāsatyas, which for three nights, three days full swiftly travelled, to the sea's farther shore, the strand of ocean, in three cars, hundred-footed, with six horses. Ye wrought that hero exploit in the ocean which giveth no support, or hold, or station, what time ye carried Bhujyu to his dwelling, borne in a ship with a hundred oars, O, As'vins" (R. V. i. 116. 3. 5). "With horses brown of hue that flew with swift wings ye brought back Bhujyu from the sea of billows. The son of Tugra had invoked you, As'vins; borne on he went uninjured through the ocean. Ye with your chariot swift as thought, well-harnessed, carried him off, O, mighty ones, to safety" (R. V. i. 117. 14. 15). "Ye came to Bhujyu, struggling in the flood, with flying birds, self-yoked, ye bore him to his sires. Ye went to the far distant home, O, mighty ones" (R. V. i. 119. 4). "For Tugra's son your car, sea-crossing, strong, was equipped and set amid the waters" (R. V. i. 158. 3). "Ye made for Tugra's son amid the water-floods that animated ship with wings to fly withal, whereon with god-devoted mind ye brought him forth, and fled with easy flight from out the mighty surge. Four ships most welcome in the midst of ocean, urged by the As'vins, save the son of Tugra, him who was cast down headlong in the waters, plunged in the thick inevitable darkness. What tree was that which stood fixed in surrounding sea to which the son of Tugra supplicating clung? Like twigs, of which some winged creature may take hold, ye As'vins, bore him off safely to your renown" (R. V. i. 182. 5. 7). "So ye, with birds, out of the sea and waters bore Bhujyu, son of Tugra, through the regions: speeding with winged steeds through dustless spaces, out of the bosom of the flood they bore him" (R. V. vi. 62. 6). "What time his wicked friends abandoned Bhujyu, O, As'vins, in the middle of the ocean, your horse delivered him, your faithful servant" (R. V. vii. 68.7). "Bhujyu, abandoned in the midst of ocean, you raised from out the water with your horses, uninjured, winged, flagging not, undaunted, with deeds of wonder, saving him, O As'vins" (R. V. vii 69. 7). "When did the son of Tugra serve you, men? Abandoned in the sea, that with winged steeds your car might fly" (R. V. viii. 5. 22). "Flying steeds brought Tugra's son" (R. V. viii. 63. 14). "Ye lifted up the son of Tugra from the floods" (R. V. x. 39. 4). "Ye twain to Bhujyu tossed about in ocean at the region's end, Nāsatyas, with your winged steeds came nigh, and gave him strength to win" (R. V. x. 143. 5). It is apparent from these passages that though merchants travelled on ships to foreign countries, the Rishis themselves were not much acquainted with shipping details or incidents of sea-voyage, except that ships were furnished with "wings". This is because they lived inland, far from the ocean though one Rishi mentions the eastern and the western ocean (R. V. x. 136. 6); they had no opportunities of becoming intimately acquainted with the ships of a hundred oars, the winged, flying steeds that scoured the sea. But the Rishis were fairly familiar with boats; the earth is said to shake at the rush of the Maruts, like a full boat, which quivering, lets the water in (R. V. v. 59. 2); the sorcerer thrusts forth his rivals "as a skilful poleman (s'ambī), a boat on the waters" (A. V. ix. 2. 6); rivals are cursed to float "like a boat severed from its mooring (bandhanam, A. V. iii. 6. 7); the kapiñjala bird is said to send out its voice as a boat is sent out by a steerman (R. V. ii. 42. 1); foemen are bidden "to drift downward like a boat torn from the rope that fastened it" (A. V. iii. 6. 7) and sacrifice is compared to a boat equipped with oars (R. V. x. 101. 2). The word, 'bridge' (setu) occurs in R. V. ix. 41. 2 and probably meant a dam or sand-bank thrown across a rivulet. Loads were carried on the shoulders of porters slung from a cross-bar to which were attached loops of rope (s'ikya A. V. xiii. 4. 8).

The chief amusement of the nobles was chariot-racing (R. V. ix. 32. 5, viii. 69. 4. 6, x. 68. 2). Three-seated (R. V. i. 35. 6) and eight-seated cars (R. V. x. 53. 7) are mentioned. The successful horses were decked and the owner received the stakes (R. V. i. 60. 5). "The generous steed was adorned for deeds of might,......to show his strength and bear each prize away" (R. V. i. 130. 6). "Coursers who have triumphed in the contest or those who, famed, have won the prize with glory," were lauded in songs. (R. V. x. 74. 1). "Symmetrical in flank, with rounded haunches, mettled like heroes," (R. V. i. 162. 10) the steeds ran the race. The incidents of the race-course provided Rishis with similes. "Yea, when the strong have entered our assembly, and singers seeking with their hymns your [Indra's] favour, they are like steeds who come into the race-course" (R. V. vii. 93. 3). Men win glory "as a car-horse might the goal" (R V. ii. 31. 7). The Maruts drip like horses in a race (R. V. ii. 34. 3). Next to racing, hunting was popular. They hunted wild elephants (R. V. x. 40. 4). They hunted also the wild boars "having tusks of iron" (R. V. i. 88. 5) with trained hounds (R. V. vii. 55. 4, x. 86. 4), wild bulls with the bow (R. V. x. 51. 6), as also the "thought-fleet" (R. V. i. 85. 4) deer (R. V. viii. 2. 6); they hunted birds with arrows or falcons (R. V. ii. 42. 2, A. V. iii. 3. 3). They caught lions (R. V. v. 74. 1) and wild bulls (g a v a y a, g a u r a, R. V. iv. 21. 8) in traps and entangled their feet in leather straps (R. V. x. 28. 10, 11). They caught birds also by means of nets stretched on poles (R. V. ii. 29. 5, A. V. viii. 8. 5—8). Other game, too, seems to have been caught similarly (R. V. i. 125. 2). The ancient Indian nobles were much addicted to gambling. Even now semi-sacramental gambling is practised in most parts of India on occasions of religious festivals. Indra is compared in the hymns to a gambler who by superior play wins advantage and piles his gains in season (R. V. x. 42. 9, x. 43. 5). He seizes the foeman's riches "like a gambler gathering his winnings" (R. V. ii. 12. 4). Gambling was not considered a sin though sires punished sons caught gambling (R. V. ii. 29. 5). On the contrary, it is mentioned as an activity similar to sacrifice and study. "If, a suppliant, I call on the gods, if we have dwelt in Vedic studentship (b r a h m a c h a r y a m), if I take up the brown dice,—let them [the Apsarases] be gracious to us in such plight." (A. V. vii. 109. 7). Some gamblers staked their wealth, their wives and even their personal freedom (R. V. x. 34. 4). The "brown dice," (a k s h a) made of the nuts of the v i b h ī t a k a (Terminalia Bellerica) were sprinkled with ghī, charms for success were muttered and hey were played with a gambling board (a d h i d e v a n a, A. V. v. 31. 6). The following is one of the many prayers for success in gambling. "As the lightning at all times smites irresistibly the tree, thus would I to-day irresistibly beat the gamesters with my dice Whether they be alert or not alert, the fortune of (these) folks, unresisting, shall assemble from all sides, the gain (collect) within my hands. I invoke with reverence Agni, who has his own riches : here attached he shall heap up gain for us! . . . I have conquered and cleaned thee out (?); I have also gained thy reserve. As the wolf plucks to pieces the sheep, thus do I pluck thy winnings. Even the strong hand the bold player conquers, as the skilled gambler heaps up his winnings at the proper time. Upon him that loves the game (the god), and does not spare his money, (the game, the god), verily bestows the delights of wealth. Through (the possession of) cattle we all would suppress (our) wretched poverty, or with grain our hunger, O, thou oft-implored (god)! may we, foremost among rulers, unharmed, gain wealth by our cunning devices! Gain is deposited in my right hand, victory in my left. Let me become a conqueror of cattle, horses, wealth and gold! O, dice, yield play, profitable as a cow that is rich in milk! Bind we to a streak of gain, as the bow (is bound) with the string!" (A. V. vii. 50). The gambling-board was marked with 53 squares (R. V. x. 34. 8), probably one central square and thirteen on each of four lines radiating from the centre in the four directions. Several technical terms connected with dice are mentioned, *e.g.*, g l a h a, pool (A. V. iv. 38. 1), ā k i r, throwing (A. V. iv. 38. 2), p r a h ā, stake (A. V. iv. 38. 3), etc. The attractions of gambling are graphically described. "Sprung from tall trees on windy heights, these rollers transport as they turn upon the table. Dearer to me the die that never slumbers than the deep draught of Mūjavān's own soma" (R. V. x. 34. 1). Gambling-houses were maintained for the use of gamesters where meat and liquor were abundantly provided (A. V. vi. 70. 1) and kings, too, "paid homage" to dice (R. V. x. 34. 8). A prayer to the Apsarases, who were the presiding goddesses of dice, asking them to forgive cheating at dice is given in the Atharva Veda (vi. 118). Dice and drinking are said in R. V. vii. 86. 6 to have led even Rishis astray. Other amusements mentioned are witnessing the combats of boxers (m u s h ṭ i k ā) with those that challenged them (R. V. iii. 20. 20), the performances of dancing women, with broidered garments and open bosoms (R. V. i. 92. 4), "robed in garments fair as heaven to look on" and displaying themselves actively, (R. V. vi. 29. 3), or men dancers who with breasts adorned with gold (R. V. viii. 20. 22) performed war-dances (R. V. v. 33. 6) and perhaps expounded, with action-songs, the deeds of heroes. Boys and girls decked with lotus-garlands (R V. x. 184. 2), swung in green and bright swings (p r e ṅ k a) and sang to the accompaniment of lutes (a g h ā t a) and cymbals (k a r k a r ī, A. V. iv. 37. 4). Other musical instruments mentioned are g a r g a r a, g o d h ā and p i ṅ g ā, the first and the last being probably stringed and the other of leather (R. V. vii. 58. 9); there was also the b ā k u r a, bag-pipe (R. V. ix 1. 8), and the drum (d u n d u b h i), described in connection with battles. The people spent much time in "songs and revels" (u k t h ā m a d ā n i, A. V. v. 26. 3); the earth (b h ū m i) is described as the place "where men sing and dance with loud noises" (v y a i l a b a, A. V. xii. 1 41). Dancing in open air was common (R. V. v. 52. 12); the gods are said to have "stood close-clasping one another" and kicked up in dancing the atoms which formed the earth, as a thick cloud of dust rises from the feet of dancers (R. V. x. 72. 6.) In the next verse these dancing gods are called y a t i s, devotees; hence we may infer that religious dancing, not unlike what is done in Bhajana parties to-day also existed.

Cattle-lifting and other kinds of thieving were the chief forms of crime. Thieves stole cows and hid in dark caves with the stolen cows (R. V. i. 65. 1). They stole garments and a hue and cry was raised after them as loud as the cry of battles (R. V. iv. 38. 5). "The robber with the gulieful heart" lurked about the highway like a wolf and the traveller prayed to the god P ū s h ā to chase him away (R. V. i. 42. 2, 3). Thieves also broke into houses in quest of treasure (R. V. viii. 29. 6). When caught they were severely punished. Their arms were tied behind the back, their mouth was bandaged (A. V. vii. 70. 5) and they were severely beaten and "crushed to bits" (A. V. iv. 3. 5). A savage form of punishment, apparently for injuring a Brāhmaṇa's cow, is described in A. V. xii. 5. 65—71. "Do thou from him, the Brahmaṇ's tyrant, criminal, niggard, blasphemer of the gods, with hundred-knotted (jointed?) discus, sharpened, edged like a razor-blade, strike off the shoulders and the head. Snatch thou the hair from off his head, and from his body strip the skin; tear out his sinews, cause his flesh to fall in pieces from his frame. Crash thou his bones together, strike and beat the marrow out of him; dislocate all his limbs and joints." There is a reference to a prison (ū r v a) in R. V. iv. 12. 5 and to fetters of iron (A. V. vi. 63. 2, p a ḍ b i s′ a, viii. 1. 4). The ordeals of fire, water and single combat seem to be referred to in the following:—"Let not the wood ten times up-piled consume me, when fixed for you it bites the ground it stands on. The most maternal streams, wherein the Dāsas cast me securely bound, have not devoured me. When Traitana would cleave my head asunder, the Dāsa wounded his own breast and shoulders" (R. V. i. 158. 4, 5).

The animal foes of man were roaring lions (R. V. ix. 64. 8), wild elephants "eating forests" (R. V. i. 64. 7), tigers, wolves and hyenas (A. V. xii. 1. 49), as well as snakes, metaphorically called "ropes with teeth" (A. V. iv. 3. 2) "brandishing as it were a club" (A. V. i. 27. 2); more than twelve species of snakes are named in the Atharva Veda Samhitā as creeping amidst grasses of which five species are named in R. V. i. 191. 3. There was also the "sharply-stinging scorpion" (A V. xii. 1. 46) of whom the Rishi sang, "No strength in thy two arms hast thou, nor in thy head, nor in thy middle; then what is that small thing thou so viciously bearest in thy tail? . . . Thou, creature, who inflictest wounds both with thy mouth and with thy tail; no poison in thy mouth hast thou; what at thy tail's root may there be?" (A. V. vii. 56. 6, 8); worms of various kinds born in the rainy season (A. V. xii. 1. 46), and the "sharply-biting" mosquito (A. V. vii. 56. 3) are also mentioned.

Life in the age of the Mantras was sufficiently organized for lands to be measured (R. V. ii. 15. 3) with measuring rods (R. V. iii. 38. 3), classified as barren (k h i l a, A. V. vii. 115. 4), waste (d h a n v ā, A. V. vii. 117. 1), forest (a r a ṇ y a, A. V. xii. 1. 11), and cultivated land (u r v a r ā, R V. viii. 80. 6), and for fields to be definitely marked out (R. V. i. 110. 5). The Atharva Veda mentions two units of measurement, the a b h ī s' u, lit., rein,—evidently a short measure and the v y ā m a, the space between the tips of the fingers when the arms are extended (vi.

137. 2). As now, some portion of the wealth of a family consisted in gold put into pitchers and buried, for the digging up of a "buried pitcher full of gold" is referred to in R. V. i. 117. 12. Property was stable enough to require laws of inheritance. Two rather obscure Mantras, placed at the head of R. V. iii. 31 and unconnected with the rest of the sūktam, deal with the subject of inheritance. "The father who has no sons honours his son-in-law, capable of begetting sons, and goes (for an heir) to the son of his daughter. The sonless father trusts in his daughter's offspring and lives content. A son does not give any of his father's property to a sister. He gives her away to be the wife of a husband. If a father and mother beget both son and daughter, the one (*i e.*, the son) engages himself in the acts and duties of his father, while the other (*i.e.*, the daughter) receives honour." After the father's death, the brother was the guardian of the unmarried sister and watched over her morals (R. V. i. 124. 7, A. V. 1. 14. 2, iv. 5. 5). The hankering for sons, so characteristic of Indians even to-day existed quite as strongly in old times. To beget a son was a debt due to one's forebears and the son was therefore the "cancellor of (the father's) debt" (R. V. vi. 61. 1). People prayed to Agni that they might live in their sons (R. V. i. 97. *i e*, 4), *i.e.*, "become immortal by (begetting) children." (R. V. v. 4. 10). Begetting children was spinning out the thread of life (A. V. x. 2. 17). Sons were preferred to daughters. There are several charms in the Atharva Veda to ensure the birth of a son, (*e.g.*, vi. 17) and to change the fœtus into a male (*e.g.*, vi. 11), the root of the pumsavaṅam ceremony of later times. As a son was regarded as alone the cancellor of the debts of the father to his forefathers, Indra is begged to vouchsafe to the newly married bride ten sons and make

her husband the eleventh man in the house (R. V. x. 85. 45) and Pinga, a yellow herb, was relied upon to drive away the demons that might turn the child in the womb into a female. Men without issue adopted sons of other people, though such adoption was untasteful. "No son is he who springs from others... Unwelcome for adoption is the stranger, one to be thought of as another's offspring, though grown familiar by continual presence." (R. V. vii 4. 7, 8). As now, sons of brothers must have quarrelled much in the old days in "parting an aged father's wealth" (R. V. i. 70. 5) among themselves, because the word bhrātṛivyāḥ, cousins, had come to mean enemies (A. V. x. 3. 9). But the relations of fathers to sons seem to have been pleasant. The father was "easy of approach to the son" (R. V. i. 1. 9). Boys bowed respectfully, *i.e.*, prostrated themselves before fathers, as now, when they met them (R. V. ii. 33. 12) and the father took the son up with both hands (R. V. i. 38. 1). When the father became old, his son protected him and kept him "gay" in his house (R. V. vi. 3. 7). Numerous similes are taken from the relations of parents to children. "As men accept a true-born infant" (R. V. iii. 15. 2), "As a mother welcomes her dear heart-gladdening son" (R. V. v. 42. 2), "As on his father's lap the son, the darling, so on the fire is set the sacred caldron" (R. V. v. 42. 7), "Like a son cherished in his father's house" (R. V. viii. 19. 27), "Greets him with cries of pleasure as a son his father" (R. V. vii. 103. 3). The obverse of the picture is found in the story of Rijrās'va, who "slew a hundred wethers for the she-wolf," in which guise, one of the asses of the As'vins appeared before him; "his father robbed Rijrās'va of his eye-sight" for this extravagance, but the As'vins, "Nāsatyas wonder-workers, physicians gave him [back his] eyes, that he saw with sight uninjured" (R. V. i. 116. 16). "He whom for furnishing a hundred wethers to the she-wolf, his wicked father blinded,—to him, Rijrās'va, gave ye eyes, O, As'vins; light to the blind ye sent for perfect vision. To bring the blind man joy thus cried the she-wolf: O As'vins, O ye mighty ones, O, heroes, for me Rijrās'va, likea youthful lover, hath cut piecemeal one and a hundred wethers" (R. V. i. 117. 17. 18). This severity of parental chastisement is in keeping with the general cruelty of the punishments of the age.

Though the birth of daughters was deprecated (A. V. vi. 11. 4.), yet women occupied an honourable position in the household. The wife took part in religious ceremonies (R. V. i. 72. 5). "Pairs waxing old in their devotion seek thee" (R. V. v. 43. 15). "Couples desirous of thine aid are storming thee, pouring their presents forth (R. V. i. 131. 3). The sacrificer and his wife are joint "deities" of one hymn (R. V. x. 183). Even to-day, the wife is associated with the husband in the fire-rites. It was more so in ancient times. "O Gods, with constant draught of milk, husband and wife with one accord press out and wash the soma juice. They gain sufficient food: they come united to the sacred grass, and never do they fail in strength. Never do they deny or seek to hide the favour of the Gods; they win high glory for themselves, with sons and daughters by their side they reach their full extent of life, both decked with ornaments of gold. Offering sacrificial meal and wealth, to become immortal (in sons and grandsons), samūdho romas'am hatah, they pay due honour to the Gods." (R. V. viii. 31. 5—9). When married, the wife took her seat at the place of sacrifice (R. V. x. 85. 24), because she was, from that moment, to be "the household's mistress and speak, as a lady, to the gathered people" (R. V. x. 85. 26) and to "bear full sway over the husband's father, the husband's mother, and his sisters and his brothers." (R. V. x. 85. 46). Ladies were not shut up in houses but went about freely. "From olden time the matron goes to feast and general sacrifice" (R. V. x. 86. 10). They "trooped to festal meetings, decked, shining forth with sunbeams" (R. V. i. 124. 8); women were "agreeable at festivals" (samana, A. V. ii. 36. 1) Ladies were very particular about their toilet; they combed their hair with combs (kaṅkata) of hundred teeth (A. V. xiv. 2. 68), "decked themselves with gay ornaments" (R. V. iv 58. 9), and wreaths of flowers (A. V. i. 14. 1) and attended gatherings "fair to look on and gently smiling" (R. V. iv. 58. 8). Fair dames "embellished their bodies" (R. V. ii. 39. 2) with garlands and scents (R. V. vii. 55. 8) and unguents (R. V. x. 85. 7), charmed away with spells inauspicious marks (hair-growths, hair-rings, etc., (A. V. i. 18. 3), and secured a wealth of hair on their heads by spells (A. V. vi. 36, etc.), and walked out "glancing" to the right and left (R. V. i. 75. 1) and smiling "like a flatterer" and rejoicing their admirers with their fair faces (R. V. i. 92. 6). "In pride of beauty, the maid walked forth, smiling, youthful, shining brightly, discovering her bosom" (R. V. i. 123. 10). Loving wives decked themselves to please their spouses (R. V. i. 124. 7), with "their breasts, hips and heads quivering with passion" (R. V. x. 86. 7), displayed their beauty to their husbands (R. V. x. 71. 4), clung to them as round the tree the wood-bine clings, girding them with hands as a girdle (R. V. x. 10. 13), and jāyā yuvate patim, tuñjāte vrishnyam payah paridāya rasam duhe (R. V. i. 105. 2). "Honourable dames, true, active workers, who knew well the morning" (R. V. i. 79. 1) were the good housewives (k u l a p ā) who rose with the dawn, because they believed that "the rising sun robs sleepers of their splendour, (A. V. vii. 13. 2) and roused the "coiled-up sleepers" (R. V. i. 113. 5), "as a fly awakens those that sleep" (R. V. i. 124. 4), set the slave-girls (d ā s ī) husking rice with wooden mortar and pestle (A. V. xii. 3. 13) called "forest-tree pressing stones" (A. V. iii. 10. 8) and churn butter out of curds with churning-staff (m a n t h ā) bound with cords as horse with reins (R. V. i. 28. 4) and set every one in the house their daily work (R. V. i. 48. 6). Women active in their tasks sang songs while working (R. V. i. 92. 3). Some ladies composed mantras and rose to the rank of Rishis, like Vis'vavārā, author of R. V. v. 28. Ghoshā, daugher of Kakshīvān, who was afflicted with dropsy and hence unmarriageable, appealed to the As'vins "Give her your aid, as sire and mother aid their son. Poor, without kin or friend or ties of blood am I. Save me, before it is too late, from this my curse." (R. V. x. 39. 6). Ghoshā further sang, "We have prepared this laud for you, O As'vins, and, like the Bhrigus, as a car have framed it, have decked it as a maid to meet her bridegroom, and brought it as a son, our stay for ever." (R. V. x. 39. 14). Ghoshā is the author of the next hymn also (R. V. x. 40), where she again lauds the As'vins as helpers of their worshippers, "Ye two assist the widow and the worshipper; and ye throw open, As'vins, unto those who win the cattle-stall that thunders with its seven-fold mouth. The woman hath brought forth, the infant hath appeared, the plants of wondrous beauty straightway have sprung up. To him the rivers run as down a deep descent, and he this day becomes their master and their lord.........Of this we have no knowledge. Tell it forth to us, how the youth rests within the chambers of the bride. Fain would we reach the dwelling of the vigorous steer who loves the kine, O As'vins: this is our desire." The As'vins granted Ghoshā her desire, for she says, "your favouring grace hath come, ye lords of ample wealth" and further asks them to "give hero sons and riches to the eloquent." Another female Rishi was Apālā, of the family of Atri and a devotee of Indra. She tells her tale in the hymn she has composed (R. V. viii. 80). "Down to the stream a maiden came, and found the Soma by the way. Bearing it to her home, she said, for Indra will I press thee out, for S'akra will I press thee out." [She then addresses Indra.] "Thou roaming yonder, hero, who beholds every house in turn, drink thou this Soma pressed with teeth, accompanied with grain and curds, with cake of meal and songs of praise. O Indra, cause to sprout again three places, these which I declare,—my father's head, his cultured field, and this the part below my waist. Make all of these grow crops of hair, yon cultivated field of ours, my body and my father's head." Indra granted Apālā her wishes, for she concludes, "cleansing Apālā, Indra, thrice thou gavest sunlike skin to her, drawn, S'atakratu, through the hole of car, of wagon and of yoke."

Many professions were open to women, such as weaving, embroidery, cane-splitting, dyeing, etc. (V. S. xxx, *op. cit.*) Daughters shared in the household work; they brought home water from wells (R. V. i. 191. 14), jars beautifully poised on their heads (A. V. x. 8. 14) and otherwise helped mothers in the household work. Girls sometimes remained unmarried in their parent's homes (R. V. ii. 17. 7) "till the hair was white with age" (A. V. i. 14. 3) but it was considered a misfortune to remain an old maid and Ghoshā, a woman stricken in years, who lived a maid in her father's dwelling, did not rest content till she gained a husband (R. V. i. 117. 7). Some married for love, maidens bowing modestly "before the gallant lover who comes with love to them who yearn to meet them" (R. V. x. 30. 6). Others married for money; "how many a maid is pleasing to the suitor who fain would marry for her splendid riches?" (R. V. x. 27. 12). The "worthless son-in-law" paid a heavy price for a wife (R. V. i. 109. 2.) As now, the daughter-in-law, modestly slunk before the father-in-law (A V. viii. 6. 24) and the unpleasant son-in-law spent evenings far from his parents-in-law to spite them (R. V. viii. 2. 22) even though the anxious mother "decked her daughter" (R. V. i. 123. 11) to attract him. Ordinarily a man married but one wife, but polygamy was not unknown. "Between both poles the car-horse goes pressed closely, as in his dwelling moves the doubly wedded man" (R. V. x. 101. 11.) A Rishi tortured with care, exclaims, "Like rival wives my ribs press painfully on me all round" (R. V. i. 105. 8). Indra is said to have taken to himself all the cities "as one common husband doth his spouses" (R. V. vii. 26. 3). When a man had two wives, each of them used spells to "quell the rival wife, and make her lower than the lowest dames" (R. V. x. 145. 1. 3). She placed beneath the husband (probably beneath his pillow), a herb of magical properties called the pāṭā, to secure the husband for herself (A. V. iii. 18. 2. 6).

Evil-disposed wives, hostile to their husbands, for whom a special hell was created by the gods (R. V. iv. 5. 5), were unfaithful to their spouses. They seem to have received lovers at their homes. There is a whole hymn (A. V. iv. 5), by means of which the paramour of an amorous lady sought to lull all the folk of the house to sleep, charm the dogs into silence and prayed to Indra to help him to escape free from scath and harm during his visit to his inamorato. Giddy girls, not well looked after by their brothers, went astray (R. V. iv. 5. 5) and fondly went to the place where they hoped to meet their lovers (R. V. x. 34. 5). Children born of illicit unions were abandoned (R. V. ii. 29. 1.); one such cast-away, the son of an unwedded damsel, Agru, was thrown into an anthill, but was saved by Indra and became a Rishi (R. V. iv. 19. 9, iv. 30. 6). Professional prostitution also existed; some women sought men, "mounting their cars to gather riches" (R. V. i. 124. 7) and "went about displaying themselves with glittering ornaments, like the heavens with stars" (R. V. i. 87. 1). The average woman was however chaste and bent her forehead down before her lord in token of chaste subjection (R. V. v. 80. 6) and a loving husband and wife are compared to the chakravāka and its mate, birds well-known for being referred to in later literature as emblems of love and constancy. (A. V. xiv. 2. 64). Good wives "cared for each one at home" (R. V. i. 66. 3) and made the house a happy place; Indra's home was of course the ideal one, so much so that he was perplexed in choosing between the attractions of home and of the soma-oblations of his worshippers. "A wife, Indra, is one's home; she is a man's dwelling; therefore let thy horses be yoked, and carry thee thither. But whenever we pour forth a libation of soma, then may Agni hasten to call thee. Depart, Indra; come hither, brother Indra; in both quarters thou hast inducements, whenever thy great chariot halts, thy steed is unharnessed. Depart, Indra, to thy home; thou has drunk the soma; thou hast a lovely house, and pleasure in thy house. Wherever thy great chariot halts, it is proper that thy steed should be unharnessed" (R. V.

iii. 53. 4. 6). The ladies that gave presents to Brāhmaṇas were of course eulogized. The fertile earth is compared to "the bounteous lady, liberal of her gifts," in R. V. v. 56. 3. The Rishi S'yāvās'va praises the pious wife of Taranta (R. V. v. 61.) "May she gain cattle for her meed, hundreds of sheep and steeds and kine, who threw embracing arms around the hero [Taranta] whom S'yāvās'va praised. Yea, many a woman is more firm and better than the man who turns away from Gods and offers not. She who discerns the weak and worn, the man who thirsts and is in want, she sets her mind upon the gods. And yet full many a one, unpraised, mean, niggard, is entitled man: only in weregild is he such. And she, the young, the joyous-spirited, divulged the path to S'yāva, yea, to me. Two red steeds carried me to Purumīlha's side, that sage of far-extended fame" (*Ib.* 5—9). Widows remarried and after death, rejoined in heaven-world that husband who in life had offered the oblation called p a ñ c h a u d a n a m (A. V. ix. 5. 27). Widows were also allowed to cohabit with the deceased husband's brother (R. V. x. 40. 2), possibly because as the brother inherited his childless brother's property, he took his wife as well, a custom still observed among sundry low castes. Women, like cattle, were regarded as a prize of war (R. V. iv. 17. 16, ix 67. 10—12). They were denounced as being of ungovernable temper and fickle mind (R. V. viii. 33. 17) and it is said that "with women there can be no lasting friendship; hearts of hyenas are the hearts of women" (R. V. x. 95. 15). The well-known khila mantra which begins with y a ṅ m e m ā t ā, and is repeated by Āpastambīyas during s'r ā d d h am and which means "wherein my mother has gone astray and done amiss, faithless to her marriage vow may my father take that r e t a s (as his own); may another one fall off from the mother" was inspired by the same contempt for women. The Rishis did not consider it ungallant that a man should war with a woman. This is how Indra's fight with Ushas, the dawn-maiden, is described. "This, Indra, was a deed of might and manliness which thou didst achieve, that thou didst smite the daughter of the sky, a woman who was bent on evil. Thou, great Indra, didst crush Ushas, though the daughter of the sky, who was exalting herself. Ushas fled away in terror from her shattered car, when the vigorous Indra crushed it." (R. V. iv. 30. 8. 10).

The ideal of feminine beauty and accomplishments according to the Vedic poets is found in Indrāṇī's description of her own charms. "There is no woman with broader bhasat than I, (T. B. ii. 4. 2. 7 says trims'at asyāh jaghanam yojanāni), none having more yās'u none (pumāmsam) prati (sarirasya atyantam) chyavīyasī none s'akthi udyamīyasī" (R. V. x. 86. 6). The picture is completed by Indra who calls her "Dame with lovely hands and arms, broad hair-plaits and broad jaghanam" (*Ib.* 8). Two Riks placed out of context at the end of R. V. I. 126. 8, refer to the same subject. Thus a man jokes with a woman. "Āgadhitā parigadhitā (svīkritā-paritogrihītā, yadvā, ā samantāt mis'ra-yantī, āntaram prajanena, bāhyam bhujā-dibhih) who like an ichneumon, holds tight, the yādurī (bahuretoyuktā), bhojyā, gives a hundred yās'ūnām (of prajananakarmāṇi.)" She replies, "Come near, (mama gopanīyam aṅgam) parāmris'a, I am all romas'a like the ewes of Gandhāra" (*Ib.* 6, 7). There is a similar dialogue in R. V. x. 86. 16. 17. Says Indrānī "na ses'e yasya rambate antarā sakthyā kaprit(s'epas), sedīs'e yasya romas'am nishedushah vijrimbhate." Indra replies, "na ses'e yasya romas'am nishedushah vijrimbhate, sedīs'e yasya rambhate antarā sakthyā kaprit." The preoccupation of the Rishis with the attractions of woman was so great that numerous metaphors and similes were drawn from the subject. "Like a maid triumphing (s'as'adānā) in her beautiful form thou (Ushas) advancest to meet" the god "who seeks after thee, smiling, youthful, resplendent, thou unveilest thy bosom in front. Like a fair girl, adorned by her mother, thou displayest thy body to the beholder" (R. V. i. 123. 10. 11). "The dawn hath been beheld like the bosom of a bright maiden" (R. V. i. 124. 4). "Thou, full of brightness, displayest thy bosom, a goddess, shining in thy glory" (R. V. xi. 64. 2). "Tree after tree, thou (Lākshā) climbest, like a lustful girl" (A. V. v. 5. 3). "Bees take honey in their mouth as a woman goes to an assignation" (R. V. x. 40. 6). "Expansive let them (the doors) open widely, like wives adorned for their husbands" (A. V. v. 12. 5). "Let the s'epas, garbhasya retodhāh, set it (as skilfully) as one (sets) the feather on the shaft" (A. V. v. 25. 1). "The horse would draw an easy car, gay hosts attract the laugh and jest, s'epo romavantam bhedau (ichchhati), the frog is eager for the flood" (R. V. ix. 112. 4). "O Pūshā, send her on as most auspicious, yasyām bījam manushyāh vapanti; yā na ūrū us'atī vis'rāyate, yasyām us'antah praharāma s'epam" (R. V. x. 85. 37). "Vardhatām s'epas tena yoshitamijjahi" (A. V. vi. 101. 1). "Wake up intelligence as when a lover wakes his sleeping love (jāra āsa satīmiva, R. V. i. 134. 3). It is even said of the Brahmachārī, vowed to chastity that he "has introduced his brihats'epas in the earth and he retas siñchati upon the surface (sānu) on the earth; by that live the four directions" (A. V. xi. 5. 12). Another hymn of this kind in which the Rishi revels in obscenity is the Āhanasya verses (A. V. xx. 136) to be recited so that the sacrificer might get offspring (A. B. vi. 36), but it is too long for quotation here. These passages form the roots of the Kāma S'āstram of latter days.

The people of old India were very hospitable to their guests. "In men's houses their doors were opened wide" for guests (R. V. i. 128. 6) and "in men's houses, the well-loved guest was glorified" (R. V. vi. 2. 7). A. V. ix. 6. 3 says, "When the host looks at his guests he looks at the place of sacrifice to the gods (*i.e.*, honouring guests is a kind of sacrifice to the gods)." The guest is elaborately compared to the sacrificial ritual, parts of his body and the honours done to him to parts of the yajña in A. V. ix. 6. As soon as a guest entered a house, the host saluted him, brought him water to wash his feet, gave him a drink (as, in later times, a bowl of beef-soup), seated him inside the house on a mat. The guest was then anointed; he then bathed and dined. A separate dwelling-room, the best in the house (R. V. i. 73. 1), furnished with couches, pillows, coverlets, etc., was assigned to him (A. V. ix. 6. 3). The guest or rather the guest-food offered with prayer was regarded as the pratyaksha brahma (A. V. ix. 6. 1). The host should eat after the guest and should reserve for the latter "what comes out of the cow", *e.g.*, milk and beef (A. V. ix. 6. 39) but it must be remembered that he alone is a proper guest who is a s'rotriya, a Brāhmaṇa well versed in the hymns (A. V. ix. 6. 37).

Men wore two cloths (p a v a s t a, A. V. iv. 7. 6); the upper one (v a v r i, A. V. ix. 10. 7), especially on ceremonial occasions, was of deer-skin (R. V. i. 166. 10). The two cloths worn were also called p a r o d h ā n a m and n ī v i (A. V. viii. 2. 16). The borders were beautifully embroidered as now. To the embroidered borders of cloth are compared the morning and the evening suns between whom S a v i t ā holds stretched the sky (R. V. i. 95. 7). Some shaved their beard (A. V. vi. 58) but others grew them (R. V. x. 26. 7). The priests shaved the head, leaving a tuft worn in a knot. The Vasishṭhas wore this knot on the right (R. V. vii. 33. 1) and others on the left. Some wore turbans (u s h n ī s h a, S. Y. S. xvi. 1). The Vasishṭhas wore white clothes, (R. V. vii. 33. 1) and others, red or blue ones. The clothes were of cotton or of wool (ū r n ā, R. V. v. 44. 11). The men seem to have been particular about bathing. Inunction with fragrant oils, so common in our days, is referred to (A V. vi. 124. 3), as also pools of water fit to bathe in R. V. x. 71. 7 and the refreshing bath after toil in A. V. vi. 115. 3. Women bathed as now in rivers or tanks. Of the dawn (u s h a s) it is said, " As conscious that her limbs are bright with bathing, she stands, as it were, erect that we may see her " (R. V. v. 80. 5). Women, after bath, wore " newly washed clothes " (R. V. ix. 69. 4), and " balmed themselves with unguents and scents, of which five kinds are named in A. V. iv. 37. 13 (g u g g u l ū, p ī l ā, n a l a d ī, a u k s h a g a n d h i, p r a m a n d i n ī). The long black locks of ladies which grow luxuriantly like reeds upon the head (A. V. vi. 137. 2, 3) were tied into knots (s t u k a, A. V. vii. 74. 2) plaited in broad plaits (R. V. x. 86. 7) and dressed in three different ways, o p a ś a (horn-like), k u r ī r a (net-like) and k u m b h a (pot-like)

(A. V. vi. 138) and decorated with flowers (A. V. iv. 5. 3). These three ways of dressing the hair can be met with now in the Punjab, Kashmir and South India respectively. Effeminate men (k l ī b a) also dressed their hair in imitation of women. (A. V. vi. 138).

Every incident in the private life of the people from before birth to after death was hedged round with ceremonial and recitation of mantras. In the earlier part of this age of the Mantras, the ceremonies were perhaps simpler than in the latter part. But in this latter part life had come so much under the influence of ceremonial that there is even found a mantra to be used as a penance for urinating in a standing posture (A. V. vii. 102). The Atharva Veda contains several mantras relating to each of the numerous incidents of a householder's life and the various wants of men and women. The existence of several mantras to secure the same end indicates that the rites were not the same in different tribes. Some at least began their daily life with the recitation of A. V. vii. 40 or 41. "Whose course all the cattle go, in whose course stand the waters, in whose course the lord of prosperity is entered—him, Sarasvān, we call to aid. We, putting on abundance of wealth [and] ambition would call hither to us Sarasvān, a bestower coming to meet his bestower, lord of prosperity, standing in wealth, seat of wealth." "Across wastes, across waters penetrated the men-beholding falcon, seeing a resting-place; passing all the lower spaces, may he come hither, propitious with Indra as companion. The men-beholding falcon, heavenly eagle, thousand-footed, hundred-wombed, vigour-giving—may he confirm to us the good that was borne away; let ours be what is in food among the fathers." Mantras influenced men's lives from birth to death. One of the means for ensuring the conception of children was the wearing of a bracelet (p a r i h a s t a) and the recitation of A. V. vi. 81. They are two p u m s a v a n a hymns, intended to make the fœtus in the womb develop into a male (A. V. iii. 23, vi. 11). The rite associated with the former consisted in breaking an arrow into pieces on the woman's head and a piece of the arrow fastened on her, symbolizing the act of p r a j a n a n a m and in pouring a few drops of a mixture of milk, mashed grain and sundry plants into her right nostril and accompanying these actions with these mantras: "Into thy womb shall enter a male germ, as an arrow into a quiver! may a man be born there, a son ten months old. A male son do thou produce, and after him a male shall be born. Thou shalt be the mother of sons, of those who are born, and those whom thou shalt bear. By the effective seed which bulls put forth do thou obtain a son; be a fruitful milch-cow. Prajāpati's work do I perform for thee: may the germ enter into thy womb. Obtain, thou, woman, a son who shall bring prosperity to thee and bring thou prosperity to him. The plants whose father was the sky, whose mother the earth, whose root the ocean, may those divine herbs aid thee in obtaining a son." A different form of the rite was associated with the other hymn referred to above. During the course of gestation charms were uttered to prevent Nirriti and her numerous brood of evil spirits from causing abortion (*e.g.*, R. V. x. 162, A. V. vi. 17). At parturition, A. V. i. 11 was muttered to secure easy child-birth. The birth-ritual was the first washing of the infant, at which, as in later times, was probably recited A. V. ii. 10 and all evil symbolically washed away from the child's body. Mantras were recited when the baby cut its first teeth and the child was fed with rice, barley, beans and sesamum (A. V. vi. 140). Fire-offerings were given for the long life of the boy(A.V. ii. 28). The boy that was to adopt the priestly profession, was consecrated for studies by tying a girdle of m u ñ j a grass round and the mantras of A. V. vi. 133, besides others were recited. He then became a B ra h m a c hā r ī, "a member of the gods' own body" (R. V. x. 109. 5), in whose glorification one whole hymn of the Atharva Veda (xi. 5) was composed. The master (ā c h ā r y a) was his (spiritual)second mother for "he takes the B ra h m a c h ā r ī into his bowels. Three nights he holds and bears him in his belly", referring to the three days' ceremony of initiation (A. V. xi. 5. 3). The boy then worshipped fire by placing logs on the sacred fire (*Ib.* 4) and was hence dedicate to the sacred lore and went about with black buck-skin, long-bearded (*Ib.* 6). He practised self-restraint during his term of studentship and studied the sacred lore (A. V. vi. 61). The sacred lore consisted of "ancient texts" (R. V. ii. 36. 6) and is called s'r u t a m in A. V. i. 1. 3. The master recited the texts and the disciple repeated them after him as frogs croak one after another (R. V. vii. 103. 5). This work of memorising mantras was done in the early morning as now (R. V. vii. 80. 1). He seems to have also learnt from books and when the period of his studentship was over, restored the book to the chest where it was deposited (A. V. xix. 72). In the case of other boys, the g o d ā n a m, performed at the age of sixteen was the first important rite. Till then the boy's locks were unshorn (R. V. vi. 75. 17). Now his hair was clipped; he poured ghī on fire, wore the clothes of an adult, was made to stand on a stone and was blessed (A. V. ii. 13); the lad thus became an adult member of the family and the tribe and one of the guardians of the family property. Women did not undergo a regular upanayanam ceremony like boys; but before they took part in sacrifices, along with their husbands, a girdle of muñja was tied round their waist, a custom mentioned both in the Taittirīya Brāhmaṇam (III. iii. 3.2-37) and the S'atapatha Brāhmaṇam (I. iii. 1. 13) and explained in the former to be the vratopanayanam or initiation of the wife into the sacred rite, while the latter explains it as intended to screen the impure part of women below the navel from the sacred fire; this new explanation was invented probably because the status of women was in the opinion of the authors of the S'atapatha Brāhmaṇam so low that they were deemed unfit for upanayanam of any kind; and as the custom was too sacred to be given up, a new explanation had to be given to it.

As brahmacharyam, studentship, the first of the stages in the life of a Brāhmaṇa, was invented in the age of the Mantras, so too, the fourth and last stage, that of the sanyāsī, called muni in the hymns. "The sounds of the shaking of the trees are like (the intonations of) munis," says R. V. vii. 56. 8. Indra is called "the friend (sakhā) of munis" (R. V. vii. 17. 14). Some munis were "wind-clad" (vātaras'anāh) and others wore "soiled garments of brown colour" (R. V. x. 136. 2). They were "long-haired" (kes'ī) and led a life of wandering. They were regarded as Gods. "The long-haired sustains fire, the long-haired (sustains) water, the long-haired (sustains) the two worlds; the long-haired is all sky to look upon; the long-haired is called this light. Munis (are) wind-clad; they wear soiled garments of brown colour; they follow the course of the wind, where the gods have gone before. Transported by our ecstasy (maunyam) we have pursued the winds. Ye mortals, behold but our bodies. The muni flies through the air, perceiving all forms, a friend fitted to secure the help of every God. The muni, impelled by the Gods, the steed of Vāta, the friend of Vāyu, dwells in both oceans, that which is in the east and that which is in the west. Moving in the path of the Apsarases, the Gandharvas, and the wild animals, the long-haired is aware of our call and a sweet and gladdening friend. Vāyu churned for him; the long-haired breaks down things which are unbending, by means of the vessel of water (v ī s h a m) which he drank along with Rudra." (R. V. x. 136). The v r ā t y a seems to have been a kind of ascetic different from the m u n i. The vrātyas were wandering sadhus, who went about in rough carts (v i p a t h a) to which were yoked two bulls driven by a charioteer armed with a goad (or whip, p r a t o d a) two fore-runners before and two footmen (p a r i s h k a n d a) behind. They grew their hair long and wore a garment and a turban (u s h n ī s h a m) and carried a bow, blue its belly and red its back and amulets (m a ṇ i). Besides there was a harlot (p u m s c h a l i) and a ministrel (m ā g a d h a) amidst the retinue. (A. V. xv. 1, 2). As to-day, sādhus, were respected almost like Gods whatever be their incapacity to be religious teachers and whatever life they lead, so, too, the vrātyas were highly venerated in Ancient India. The vrātya "became great, became the great God" (A. V. xv. 1) and Bhava, S'arva, Is'āna, Rudra, and Mahādeva were regarded as his attendants (A. V. xv. 5). Evidently the vrātyas were devotees of S'iva. Kings honoured them (A. V. xv. 10) and Brāhmaṇas welcomed them as honoured guests. (A. V. xv. 12).

The first important rite in the life of girls was marriage. An unmarried girl was called "the bride of Yama" (A. V. i. 14. 2) and to remain unmarried till death was regarded as a curse. An imprecatory mantra says, "May she long sit with her relatives until her hair drops from her head," *i e.*, becomes bald with age. (A. V. i. 14. 3). Hence when girls reached the marriageable age (which is not specified, but was certainly long past their childhood), charms were uttered to help to secure husbands (A. V. ii. 36). Matches were generally arranged by go-betweens. "With forelock loosened over his brow here comes the 'wooer' (a r y a m ā), the man in search of a wife for his friend, in quest of a husband for this bride, a wife for this unmarried man." (A. V. vi. 60. 1). Young suitors, sons of wealthy houses, decked their bodies with golden ornaments and accompanied the "wooer" or go-between. The mantras of the marriage-rite are found in a well-known sūktam, called Sūryā's wedding (R V x. 85). A. V. xiv. also deals with the same subject and is more elaborate. The main details of the rite can be inferred from them but we cannot be certain in what order they occurred ; no doubt, as now, various tribes arranged them in different ways. The following description follows to some extent the order in which the mantras are arranged in A. V. xiv. The bride wearing a beautiful robe (v ā s a s) and a coverlet (u p a b a r h a ṇ a m), eyes daubed with unguents (a b h y a ñ j a n a m), head dressed up in the o p a s' a or k u r ī r a styles, started for the house of her intended lord in a canopied chariot accompanied by bridal friends (a n u d e y ī). Her treasure-chest (k o s' a) containing her dowry was also placed in her chariot (xiv. i. 6-13). The following benediction was pronounced on her when she left her father's house. "Worship we pray to Aryamā, finder of husbands, kindly friend. As from its stalk a cucumber, from here I loose thee, not from there. Hence and not thence I send her free: I make her softly fettered there, that, bounteous Indra, she may live blest in her fortune and her sons.

Now from the noose of Varuna I free thee, wherewith the blessed Savitā has bound thee. In the home of righteousness, in the world of virtue, be it pleasant for thee, accompanied by the wooer. Let Bhaga take thy hand and hence conduct thee. Go to the house to be the household's mistress, and speak as a lady to thy gathered people." (*Ib.* 17-20). On the morning of the marriage she was bathed in water consecrated with mantras (*Ib.* 37-38), a yoke was held over her head (*Ib.* 40). She was then dressed with the repetition of *Ib.* 44; the mother shed tears on the impending parting from her daughter (*Ib.* 46) and the actual wedding rite began. The bride was made to stand on a stone, to represent "the lap of earth" (*Ib.* 47), the bridegroom took her hand muttering (*Ib.* 48-51,) and promised to cherish her (*Ib.* 52). He then gave her robes and jewels with which she was invested (*Ib.* 53-55). The bridegroom expressed his rapture at the sight of the newly be-robed and bejewelled bride (*Ib.* 56) and after saying some prayers to drive away demons (*Ib.* 59) and blessing a chariot (60-64), they started on the marriage procession. Mantras were muttered while the procession was going round (xiv. 2-11) to the effect that the bride was first wife of Soma, then of the Gandharva, then of Agni and Agni bestowed her on her husband and invoking the blessings of the Gods on her. Mantras were recited (*Ib.* 12-18) when the procession returned to the house of the bridegroom from where demons were exorcised (*Ib.* 19); she entered the house, then sat with her husband before the household fire (*Ib.* 20), covered with a wrapper presented to her (*Ib.* 21); she sat on a buckskin on which was spread the b a l b u j a grass (*Ib.* 22-23) and worshipped Agni along with her husband (*Ib.* 24). The husband and wife were then blessed " Let there come forth from the lap of this mother animals of various forms,.

being born; as one of excellent omen, sit thou by this fire; with thy husband be thou serviceable to the gods here. Of excellent omen, extender of houses, very propitious to thy husband, wealful to thy father-in-law, pleasant to thy mother-in-law, do thou enter these houses. Be thou pleasant to fathers-in-law, pleasant to husband, to houses, pleasant to all this clan; pleasant unto their prosperity be thou. Of excellent omen is this bride; come together, see her; having given her good fortune, go asunder and away with ill-fortunes. What evil-hearted young women, and likewise, what old ones, [are] here, do ye all now give splendour to her; then go asunder and away home" (*Ib.* 25—29). At night she was conducted to the bridal bed, where the bride and bridegroom anointed each other's eyes (*Ib.* vii. 36), and the bride invested her husband with her "m a n u-born garment" (*Ib.* vii. 37) and the bride was told, "Mount the couch with favouring mind; here give birth to progeny for this husband; like Indrāṇi, waking with a good awakening, mayest thou watch to meet dawns tipped with light. The gods in the beginning lay with their spouses; they embraced (s a m s-p ṛ i s′ a n t a) bodies with bodies; like Sūryā, O woman, all formed, with greatness, having progeny, unite (s a m-b h a v a) here with thy husband" (*Ib.* iv. 2. 31—32). Then Vis′vāvasu, the Gandharva attached to unmarried girls, was prayed to go away from her (*Ib.* 33—36) and the following mantras were recited. "Unite, O ye two parents, the two things that are seasonable; ye shall be mother and father of r e t a s; as a male a female, a d h i r o h a y a e n ā m, make ye two progeny; here enjoy wealth. Send, O Pūshā, her, most propitious, in whom men scatter r e t a s; who, eager, ū r ū v i s′ r a y ā t i; in whom we, eager, p r a h a r e m a s′ e p a h. Ā r o h a ū r u m, apply the hand, embrace thy wife with a well-willing mind ; make ye two progeny here, enjoying ; let Savitā make for you a long life-time. Let Prajāpati generate progeny for you two ; let Aryamā unite [you] with days and nights ; not ill-omened, enter thou this world of thy husband ; be weal to our bipeds ; weal to [our] quadrupeds" (*Ib.* 37—40). The nuptial garment was, the next day, presented to the Brahman priest, so that demons might go away with that robe (41-50); numerous benedictions were uttered on the newly-wedded couple (51-71); the husband finally welcomed his wife with "I am this man, that dame art thou. I am the psalm, thou the verse. I am the heaven and thou the earth. So will we dwell together, parents of children yet to be. Unmarried men desire to wed; bountiful givers wish for sons. Together may we dwell with strength unscathed, for high prosperity." (*Ib.* 71-72).

The daily life of the householder was honeycombed with magical practices. Every trouble, every disease was attributed to demons and to the witchcraft of enemies, and a foeman's thoughts were believed to hit a man like an arrow (A. V. i. 21. 4). Inherited disease was expelled by waving "a straw of barley, tawny brown, with its silvery ears" (A. V. ii. 8. 3). Water was consecrated with mantras (A. V. ii. 3) and sprinkled to expel evil spirits and to cure disease. Amulets (m a ṇ i) were worn to avert the evil eye (A. V. iv. 9. 6) and to ward off illness. These amulets were of lead (A. V. i. 16.), of gold (A. V. i. 35), of jaṅgiḍa, which was regarded as a panacea (A. V. ii. 4) and of mother-of-pearl set in gold (A. V. iv. 10.). A most powerful amulet which ensured long life and general prosperity was the t r i v r i t a, made of three strands of gold, three of silver and three of iron (A. V. v. 28). This probably afterwards became the 'holy thread' of the higher castes, the yajñopavītam being but a deer skin or a cloth worn round the left shoulder even in the age of the Brāhmaṇams (Tait. Āraṇ ii. i). Sorcery was the most powerful weapon used to secure all desires and it differed from sacrifices in this—that in the latter the spiritual powers were praised but in the former coerced. Even gods were within the sway of spells; Indra was allured by an Āsurī girl (A. V. vii. 38. 2) and he wore an amulet to increase his royal might and Varuna wore one for its aphrodisiac properties (A. V. iv. 4. 1). So human kings resorted to sorcery for the same purposes. Spells made kings "of lion-aspect, able to devour all the clans; of tiger-aspect, able to bend down the foe" (A. V. iv. 22. 7). The following is one of the many magical rites for conquering enemies. Fire was produced from a fire-drill, with the recitation of "Let Indra, the twirler, twirl, he, the mighty hero, fort-splitter, in order that we may slay by thousands the armies of our enemies" (A. V. viii. 8. 1). Some old rope was placed near the sparks with, "Let the putrid rope, breathing on, make yonder army putrid;" and when smoke and fire appeared, was muttered, "seeing afar smoke, fire, let our enemies set fear in their hearts" (*Ib.* 2). Fuel was placed on the fire, with "Crush yonder men out, O As′vattha, devour them speedily, O Khadira, let them be broken like the castor-oil plant; let vadhaka slay them with deadly weapons" (*Ib.* 3). In this mantra, there is a series of puns, *e.g.*, khād and Khadira, bhañja and tājadbhaṅga, vadhaka and vadha; the practices of the Atharva Veda relied much on such puns for their magical efficiency. Then various symbolic objects were strewn on the tracks of the enemy, to wit, nets, traps, stakes and mantras 4—16 of the same Sūktam were recited, an oblation was offered with mantras 17—23 and finally the magician recited the final one, "On this side conquer thou; on this side conquer away, conquer completely, conquer; hail, let these here conquer, let those yonder be conquered; hail to these!" When people wanted to injure individuals, an image (k r i t y ā) was made "like a bride at a wedding" (A. V. x. 1. 1), "having a head, having a nose, having ears" (*Ib.* 2); it was bathed (*Ib.* 9), rolled like a horse on the ground (*Ib.* 19), cut up (*Ib.* 21) or anointed, smeared and well-adorned and buried or thrown on water (*Ib.* 25. 32). Sorcery was used for other purposes also. "To whom I owe a debt, whose wife I approach, to whom I go begging, O gods, let them not speak words superior to me; ye two Apsarases, wives of gods, take notice" (A. V. vi. 118. 3). The demons who were worsted by spells were of various classes: (1) Celestial demons, the enemies of the gods, the Asuras The word Asura originally meant a powerful celestial being and was early applied to good and bad beings alike; but later on was restricted to the bad demons. (2) Rākshasas of animal forms (R. V. vii. 104. 20. 22), and Yātudhānas, eaters of the flesh of men and horses (R.V. x. 87. 17, 18). (3) Pis'āchas, eaters of corpses A. V. v. 29. 9). The greatest demon enemies of men and women were the Succubi and Incubi. "Arāti, I know thee well, as oppressor, one who penetrates. Oft, coming as a naked girl thou hauntest people in their sleep, baffling the thought, Arāti, and the firm intention of a man," (A. V. v. 7 7-8). "Let neither fiend of evil name Alins'a, Vatsapa, desire thy pair of husband-wooers (breasts, p a t i v e d a n a) which thy mother cleansed when thou wert born. . . . . Approach her not, come out hitherward, creep not thou in between her thighs. . . . The black and hairy Asura, tuft-born, also snouted, the niggards, from this girl we drive, from her pudenda, from her buttocks." (viii. 6. 1, 3, 5). Bad omens also were averted also by spells(A. V. vi. 27, 28, xi 2. 11) and rats, moles, boring beetles and other domestic pests charmed away similarly (A. V. vi. 50). Foul forms of necromancy, corresponding to the practices of the Aghorapanthīs of modern days also existed. A. V. viii. 3. 15 refers to "the sorcerer that smears himself with the flesh of men, horses and cattle."

The people that did not follow the fire-ritual and worship Indra as the king of the gods formed the majority of the population but as none of the "many languages and varied rites" (A. V. xii. i. 45) sought literary expression, we know nothing about them. No doubt their rites were exactly like the forms of worship observed by the Sudras and lower castes to-day. The householder who followed the fire-rite, lighted the sacred fire in the morning, offered daily three libations of soma in the morning to Agni, in the midday to Indra, the Maruts and the Visve Devas, and in the evening to the Ribhus (A. V. vi. 47, 48) and walked round the fire from left to right (in the way of the sun, pradakshiṇam) and bowed to it (A. V. vii. 50. 3). The soma was pressed between two stones and the juice squeezed out; it was then "cleansed with gold" (R. V. ix. 86. 43), *i.e.*, stirred with gold-ringed fingers. Then "like a fair youth who decorates his body, a courser rushing to the gain of riches, a steer to herds, so, flowing to the pitcher, he with a roar passed to the beakers" (R. V. ix. 96. 20). He was then "balmed with milk" and "a chanter well-skilled in song" (*Ib.* 22) sung his praises "as a lover sings to his darling" (*Ib.* 23) The soma-juice was then allowed to settle in the goblets "as a bird flies and settles in the forest" (*Ib.* 23) and was then offered to Indra, along with dhānā, karambha and apūpa. The following hymn (R. V. iii. 52) refers to the three daily soma oblations. "Indra, accept at break of day our soma mixed with roasted corn, with groats, with cake, with eulogies. Accept, O Indra, and enjoy the well-dressed sacrificial cake; oblations are poured forth to thee. Consume our sacrificial cake, accept the songs of praise we sing, as he who wooes accepts his bride. Famed from of old, accept the cake at our libation poured at dawn, for great, O Indra, is thy power. Let roasted corn of our mid-day libation, and sacrificial cake here please thee, Indra, what time the lauding singers, keen of purpose and eager as a bull, with hymns implore thee. At the third sacrifice, O thou whom many praise, give glory to the roasted corn and holy cake. With offered viands and with songs may we assist thee, sage, whom Vāja and the Ribhus wait upon. The groats have we prepared for thee with Pūshā, corn for thee, Lord of bay steeds, with thy horses. Eat thou the meal-cake, banded with the Maruts, wise hero, Vritra-slayer, drink the soma. Bring forth the roasted corn to meet him quickly, cake for the bravest hero mid the heroes. Indra, may hymns accordant with thee daily strengthen thee, Bold one, for the draught of soma."

The soma oblation was frequently associated with animal sacrifice. The animal was bound, killed, and its v a p ā, (great omentum) given to the gods (R. V. v. 43. 7). At the time of the oblations, the gods were invoked by their secret names (R. V. ix. 95. 2), for, otherwise, the oblations would not reach them (R. V. v. 5. 10). Occasionally the house-holder, his wife and children offered cooked rice (o d a n a m), and flesh sprinkled with ghī, and soma, distributed them to Brāhmaṇas and sought thereby to drive demons and secure the blessings of the gods. One of these offerings, called the V i s h ṭ a r ī, is extolled in A. V. iv. 34. "The b r a h m ā is its head, the b r i h a t its back, the v ā m a d e v y a m the belly of the rice-mess; the metres the sides, truth its mouth, the V i s h ṭ a rī, a sacrifice born out of fervour. Boneless, purified, cleansed with the purifier, bright, they [who offer the V i s h ṭ a rī] go to a bright world; Jātavedas burns not away their s'i s'n a m [when they are cremated after death]; in the heavenly world much women-folk is theirs. Whoso cook the V i s h ṭ a r ī rice-mess, ruin fastens not on them at any time. [Such a one] stays with Yama, goes to the gods, revels with the soma-drinking Gandharvas. Whoso cook the V i s h ṭ a r ī rice-mess, them Yama robs not of their r e t a s; becoming chariot-owner, [such a one] goes about upon a chariot-road; becoming winged, he goes all across the skies. This, extended, is of sacrifices the best carrier; having cooked the V i s h ṭ a r ī, one has entered the sky; the bulb-bearing lotus spreads, the b i s a, s'ā t u k a, s' a p h a k a, m u l ā l ī; let all these streams come unto thee, swelling honeyedly in the heavenly world; let complete lotus-ponds approach thee. Having pools of ghī, having slopes of honey, having strong drink (s u r ā) for water, filled with milk, with water, with curds, let all these streams come unto thee, swelling honeyedly in the heavenly world; let complete lotus-ponds approach thee. Four vessels, four-fold, I give, filled with milk, with water, with curds, let all these, streams come unto thee, swelling honeyedly in the heavenly world; let complete lotus-ponds approach thee. This rice-mess I deposit in the Brāhmaṇas, the V i s h ṭ a r ī, world-conquering, heaven-going; let it not be destroyed for me, swelling with s v a d h ā; be it a cow of all forms, milking my desire." A more elaborate rite of presenting Brāhamaṇas with cooked rice as fee was the Brahmaudanam; the mantras of this rite are found in A. V. xii. 3 and xi. 1. A vessel full of water was placed on a skin; the sacrificer, then his wife and then his children stepped on the skin and seated themselves there. They turned to the east, walked around the vessel and then the water-vessel was placed on the ground. Then a mortar, a pestle and a winnowing basket were placed on the skin and consecrated as before. The sacrificer took hold of his wife's hand and touched the grain to be used in the rite. The grain was then husked and winnowed. A pot was then anointed, fire was placed around it, the grain was poured into it, two blades of darbha placed on the grain and water poured. The fire was praised when the food was cooking. A few blades of darbha were strewn on the ground near the fire and a wooden platter and a ladle were placed thereon. The pot of cooked food was then taken down and put down to the west of the fire. The food was ladled out of the pot and placed in the platter. Ghī, milk and honey were poured. The husband and wife took hold of each other's hands and some benedictory mantras were then recited. The food, a home-spun garment and gold were given to Brāhmaṇas. A. V. xi. 1 refers to a similar offering. A slightly more elaborate rite was the Aja Pañchaudanam. A goat was seized, his feet carefully washed, his joints cut up neatly with "the grey knife," cooked in caldrons, and was at the same time bidden to go to the third heaven where dwell the righteous (A. V. ix. 5. 1—13). Five gold pieces, five new garments and five kine were given as fee to the priest at this sacrifice (A.V.ix.5.25). More pious people did the S'ataudanam in which a hundred pots of boiled rice were given away (A. V. ix. 9) and several animals sacrificed. A dog sacrifice by the gods is mentioned in A. V. vii. 5. 5, but nothing more is known about it. Sacrifices were offered on New moon and Full-moon days (A. V. vii. 79, 80, 81). The New moon was greeted with, "Ever new art thou, being born; sign of the days, thou goest to the apex of the dawns; thou disposest their share to the gods as thou comest; thou stretchest out, O moon, a long life-time" (A. V. vii. 81. 2), a mantra used in benedictions in modern ritual. The Full moon was greeted with, "Full behind, also full in front, up from the middle hath she of the Full moon been victorious; in her, dwelling together with the gods, with greatness, may we revel together with food on the back of the firmament" (A. V. vii. 80. 1). The dark night of the A m ā v ā s y ā was lauded with, "The night hath come, assembler of good things, causing sustenance, prosperity, [and] good to enter in; we would worship A m ā v ā s y ā with oblation; yielding sustenance with milk is she come down to us" (A. V. vii. 79. 3). Two annual festivals are referred to: the harvest festival in which good goblins called U p o h a and S a m ū h a, attendants of Prajāpati, were praised (A. V. iii. 24) and the new year festival which seems to have been celebrated on the eighth day after the Full-moon when the year commenced. This day was called e k ā s h ṭ a k ā, "the model (p r a t i m ā) of the year (A. V. iii. 10. 3). The soma juice was offered to the goddess Night, the lords of the seasons and other gods were worshipped (A. V. iii. 10).

The public rites of the fire-cult were much more elaborate than the domestic rites. In the age of the mantras the rites had become so elaborate that numerous classes of priests were required (R. V. ii. 1-2). Sacrifices extending for nine and ten months (R. V. v. 45. 7, 11) year-long rites (R.V. vii. 103. 8), and sacrificial sessions (S a t t r a) are referred to (A. V. i. 30. 4) and numerous details of long, complicated sacrifices, *e.g.*, anuyāja, prayāja, (texts and oblations of somayāga, A. V. i. 30. 4), nivid, invocations, (A. V. v. 26. 4), trikadruka (the first three days of the abhiplava festival, R. V. ii. 11. 17), the 36 grahas (pots for holding soma) of the agnishṭoma and 4 of the atyagnishṭoma, R. V. x. 114. 6) are mentioned, thus proving that before the close of the age when mantras were composed, the public (s'rauta) rites had been fully elaborated. The chief public rite was the soma sacrifice King Soma, as the plant was called, was brought into the sacrificial shed and numerous songs in its praise were sung (R. V. ix. 10. 6). Seven adhvaryus sprinkled it with water (R. V. ix. 10.7). It was crushed between two stones placed on ox-hide (R. V. ix. 101.11) or pounded in a mortar with a pestle (R. V. i. 28. 3. 4). It was then placed on a sieve and pressed (R. V. ix. 12 5); the "brown" juice was then strained through a woollen cloth (R. V. ix. 13.6) The atharvaṇa priest poured milk on it (R. V. ix. 11.2) and stirred it well with the ten fingers (R. V. ix. 8-4). It was then poured into wooden vats (R. V. ix. 33. 2) and placed on the altar (vedi, R. V. v. 31.12). After being offered to the gods (R. V. ix. 42.2, etc.), it was distributed in bowls to the priests who were gathered round, "like flies on honey" (R. V. vii. 32.2). The soma offering was made three times in the day and along with each oblation a meal-cake (puroḍās a) was also offered (R V. iii. 28). Sometimes the soma was mixed with meal, cooked and offered (R. V. iii. 32. 2). Indra was the great god who drank enormous quantities of soma. His mother gave it to him on the day of his birth (R. V. iii. 32.9) and he could drink thirty bowls at one draught (R. V. viii. 66.4). Soma-draughts resorted to him as birds to a leafy tree, flew to him as waters to the ocean or rivulets to a lake (R. V. x. 43. 4, 7). Soma inspired much of the poetry of the Rishis. The wise "milk the thundering, unfailing stalk" (R. V. ix. 72.6.) "Like cars that thunder on their way, like coursers eager for renown, have soma-drops flowed forth for wealth" (R. V. ix. 10.1). "The Somas deck themselves with milk, as kings are graced with eulogies" (R. V. ix. 10.3). "These rapid soma streams have stirred themselves to motion like strong steeds, like cars, like armies hurried forth. Swift as wide winds they lightly move, like rain-storms of Parjanya, like the flickering flames of burning fire" (R. V. ix. 22. 1, 2). "Directed by the sisters ten, (*i.e*, the fingers that stir the juice), this steer runs onwards to the wooden vats" (R. V. ix. 28.4). "Now like a swan he maketh all the company sing each a hymn: he, like a steed, is bathed in milk. O Soma, viewing heaven and earth, thou runnest like a darting deer, set in the place of sacrifice. The cows have sung with joy to him, even as a woman to her love; he came as to a settled race" (R. V. ix. 32. 3—5.) The soma juice "glideth forth like a serpent from his ancient skin, and like a playful horse the tawny steer hath run" (R. V. ix. 86. 44). The bowls from which men drunk soma led to the conception of the sky as the "bowl with mouth inclined and bottom upward" (A. V. x. 8. 9 ; the sky and the earth were "two great bowls which met, each of the pair laden with treasure" (R. V. iii. 55. 20). Associated with the s o m a y ā g a was the sacrifice of animals. The y ū p a (stake), eulogized as sovereign of the forest, (v a n a s p a t i), was placed on sacred grass (A. V. xii. 3. 33), consecrated (R. V. iii. 8. 5), decorated with rings and garlands (R.V. iii. 8. 4, 10), and colours of various tints (R. V. i. 92. 5) and "arrayed in brilliant colour" (R. V. iii 8. 9) and set up to the east of the fire (*Ib.* 1). The victim was tied to the stake with bands, "above, between and under" (R. V. i. 24. 15), *i.e.*, the head, the waist and the feet were tied; it was then anointed with ghī, robed and decked (A. V. ix. 5. 14), all the "nine holes" of its body were stopped and it was beaten on its testes till it died. The animal was taken down, placed on a dresser, carefully cut, the several parts being named and praised during the cutting (A. V. ix. 4. 11, R. V. i. 162. 18), and joints skilfully separated; the meat was then cooked and offered to the gods and eaten by the worshippers (R. v. i. 162. 11, 12). The horse sacrifice of the earlier years of the age of the mantras was a much simpler affair than the gorgeous but revolting a s'v a m e d h a of later days. In front of the horse was led a dappled goat, besides an oblation and the horse was covered with costly trappings and otherwise decorated (R. V. i. 162. 1, 2). Both were led round three times (*Ib.* 3). The priests carried the y ū p a with a carved knob and cooking vessels, (*Ib.* 6). The horse was provided with halter, heel-ropes, head-stall and girths and was baited with grass to the place of sacrifice. The horse was tied to the stake, anointed, robed and sacrificed and eaten like other animals (R.V. i. 162. 11—19). It was believed that the sacrificial victim did not die but went to the gods (R. V. i. 162. 21, A. V. ix. 5. 8). The u c h c h h i s h ṭ a or sacrificial residue was believed to be charged with the influence of all the gods invoked and is lauded in one hymn, A. V. xi. 7. There is a reference in the R i g V e d a S a m h i t ā, to a man, S'unaḥs'epa, who was bound to the stake for being sacrificed, but escaped by composing hymns (R. V. i. 24—30) to Varuṇa and other gods. Later sacrificial literature contains the ritual of human sacrifice, a copy of the later horse sacrifice, and hence such sacrifices must have existed in the earlier age of the mantras. But from the extreme paucity of the references to this subject, we must conclude that they were very rare.

These rites, some of them extending over long periods of time could not have been performed without some advance in the measurement of time. Atharva Veda x. 2·20. tells us that Purusha, primeval man, "measured out the year." As in ancient Babylonia, the year was divided into twelve months and an occasional intercalary month was added. "Formed with twelve spokes, by length of time unweakened rolls round the heaven this wheel of enduring order" (R. V. i. 164. 11). Each month had thirty days and the year 360 days or 720 days and nights. The path of the sun or the moon was regarded as divided into 30 domains (d h ā m a n, A. V. vi. 31. 3). "Herein established, joined in pairs together, seven hundred sons and twenty stand, O Agni" (R. V. i 164. 11). "The twelve-spoked wheel, for that is not to be worn out, revolves greatly about the sky of righteousness; there, O Agni, stood the suns, paired, seven hundred and twenty" (A. V. ix. 9. 13). "Twelve fellies, one wheel, three naves, who understands that? Therein are inserted three hundred and sixty pins (s' a ṅ k u), pegs (k h ī l a) that are immovable. This, O Savitā, do thou distinguish; six twins, one sole-born" (A. V. x. 8. 4,5). The day was divided into 30 (Indian) hours, these being the 30 steps taken by Ushas (R. V. vi. 59.6), Ushas being supposed to travel the 30 y o j a n a s of the sky in that time (R V. i. 123-8). The night was also thirty (Indian) hours long, these being divided into 4 watches (y ā m a m, A. V. vi. 21.2). The year was also divided into three seasons of four months each, the "three naves" of the previous passage and also into six seasons of two months each. These six seasons are named in A. V. vi. 55. 2, and xii. 1. 36, grīshma, hemanta, s'is'ira, vasanta, s'arad, varsha. The curious names naidāgha, torrid, kurvanta, making, samyanta, gathering, pinvanta, fattening, udyanta, up-going, and abhibhuva, overcoming, are found in A. V. ix. 5. 31—36. Sometimes the dewy and cold seasons were counted as one and then the seasons were taken as five. "They call him in the farther half of heaven, the five-footed, of twelve forms, wealthy in watery store. These others say that he, God with far-seeing eyes, is mounted on the lower seven-wheeled, six-spoked car. Upon this five-spoked wheel revolving ever all living creatures rest and are dependent. Its axle, heavily laden, is not heated: the nave from ancient times remains unbroken. The wheel revolves, unwasting, with its felly; ten draw it, yoked to the far-streching pole. The sun's eye moves encompassed by the region: on him dependent rest all living creatures." (R. V. i. 164, 12-14). It is not clear what the "seven wheels" and the "ten" (horses) are. Occasionally a thirteenth month was intercalated to prevent the seasons from revolving all round the year. This, too, was a month of 30 days. "He who metes out the thirteenth month, constructed with days and nights, containing thirty members, this God is wroth" (A. V. xiii. 3. 8). True to his holy law, he (Varuna) knows the twelve moons with their progeny (*i.e.*, days); he knows the moon of later birth" (R. V. i. 25. 8). "Of the coborn (the two months that make up a season) they call the seventh single-born; the six twin pairs are called Rishis, children of the gods" (R. V. i. 164. 15). "The one (sun) shines upon all creation, the other (moon) establishing the seasons is born anew" (R. V. x. 85. 18). The division of the years into twelve months implies the division of the sky into twelve "houses of the sun." This is alluded to in R. V. x. 138. 6, where Indra is said to have ordained the course of the months in the sky and divided the circumference (pradhi) of the father (sky). The names of the months are given in the Vājasaneya Samhitā. "madhu and mādhava, forming the vasanta season, s'ukra and s'uchi the grīshma, nabhas and nabhasya, the varsha, isha and ūrja, the s'arad, saha and sahasya, the hemanta, and tapas and tapasya, the s'is'ira, (vii. 30, T. S iv. 4. 12). The thirteenth month is called amhaspati in the Yajur Veda and sanisrasa, weakling, in A. V. v. 6. 4. The sun was believed to revolve round the earth, to pass the "lower space" at night and return in the morning. (A. V. vii. 41. 1). The cycle of 5 years referred to in A. V. viii. 8.23 was perhaps the period in which one intercalary month (or perhaps two) was added. The names of each of the 5 years of the cycle are given in S. Y. S. xxvii. 45 and xxx. 15 They are Samvatsara, Parivatsara, Idāvatsara, Idvatsara and Vatsara. Nakshatras (constellations) are referred to in R.V. i. 50. 2, where it is said that they," like thieves, slink away at night, before the sun who illuminates everything." "The moon is placed in the lap (upastha) of these nakshatras" (R. V. x. 85. 2); here the word nakshatra means a lunar mansion and not a star as it does in R. V. x. 88. 13 where Agni is called "an ancient nakshatra, wandering for ever, lofty, and strong, chief of Yakshas," and in R. V. x. 68. 11, where the Fathers are said to have decorated the heaven with nakshatras, as a steed is adorned with pearl. The twenty seven nakshatras or lunar mansions are referred to in a stray rik used in the chariot-racing ceremony which forms part of the vājapeya sacrifice. It says, "It was the wimd, or it was thought, of the Gaṇdharvas twenty-seven, these at the first harnessed the horse (*i.e.*, the moon): they set the power of speed in him" (S. Y. S. ix. 7). The twenty-eight lunar mansions, beginning with the K r i t t i k a s, and including A b h i j i t are named in A. V. xix. 7, T. S iv. 4. 10). Two ot them, or rather the month when the full moon is in them, are named in R. V. x. 85. 13. "In the A g h ā s, the cows are killed, in the A r j u n ī s, is the wedding." In the corresponding passage in A. V. xiv. 1. 13, the names are M a g h ā s, P h a l g u n ī s. The names of the seven stars that form the K r i t t i k a s are given in T. S. iv. 4. 5, A m b ā, D u l ā, N i t a t n i h, A b h r a y a n t ī, M e g h a y a n t ī, V a r s h a y a n t ī, C h u p u ṇ ī k ā. Stars, not lunar mansions, are also mentioned; the Heavenly Hound, and k ā l a k a ñ j a s of A. V. vi. 80 are probably Sirius and the three stars in the belt of Orion. The v i c h r i t a u, unfasteners, of A. V. vi. 110.2, are the terminal pair of the tail of the Scorpion. The milky way (r a s ā) is mentioned in A. V. iv. 2. 5. and probably in S. Y. S. xxv. 12. The distance from the earth to the heaven is said to be one thousand days' continuous journey for a golden-hued Hamsa (A. V. x. 8. 18). Astronomy was fairly well-cultivated in the age of the mantras, as the S. Y. S. xxx. mentions the professions of the star-gazer (n a k s h a t r a d a r s'a) and calculator (g a ṇ a k a).

When a man died, mantras (A. V. vii. 53) were recited to revive him; when this failed, funeral rites were started. The details of the funeral rites must, like those of the marriage rites, have differed among different tribes; nor are the mantras of the ceremony arranged in the order of their occurrence in R. V. x. 14—19, and A. V. Bk. xviii where they are collected : but the main incidents of the rite can easily be guessed from the mantras themselves. The corpse was washed (A. V. v. 19. 14) and the big toes tied together with a bunch of twigs, (called kūdī) lest death should walk back to the house after the corpse was sent out (A. V. v. 19. 12). The corpse was removed to the burning-ground accompanied not only by the mourning relatives but by professional mourners, "women of dishevelled locks," "evil-wailers" (A. V. viii. 1. 19, "weepers of evil with dishevelled hair" (A. V. xi. 2. 11). The body was removed in a cart drawn by two bulls. "I yoke for thee these two conveyers, to convey thee to the other life ; with them to Yama's seat and to the assemblies go thou down" (A. V. xviii. 2 56, T. A. iv. 1. 3). This mantra is still recited in the funeral rites through men now carry corpses to the burning ground. In the burning ground the corpse was dressed for cremation, with, "This garment hath now come first to thee ; remove that one which thou didst wear here before ; knowing, do thou follow along with what is offered and bestowed, where it is given thee variously among men of various connection." (A. V. xviii. 2. 57). The face of the corpse was covered with the omentum of a cow, with, "Wrap about thee of kine a protection from the fire ; cover thyself with grease and fatness, lest the bold one, (Agni) exulting with violence, shake thee strongly about, intending to consume thee" (A. V. xviii. 2. 58). Then his staff, if he was a Brāhmaṇa, and his bow, if a Kshatriya, were taken from the hands of the deceased one (A. V. xviii. 2. 59,60). His wife was then made to lie down on the funeral pile by the side of her husband. Unwidowed dames adorned with balm and unguent, and decked with fair jewels, then went near the corpse, (R. V. x. 18. 7) and said, "Choosing her husband's world, O man, this woman lays herself down beside thy lifeless body, preserving faithfully the ancient custom. Bestow upon her here both wealth and offspring. Rise, come up to the world of life. O woman, he is lifeless by whose side thou liest. Wifehood with this thy husband was thy portion, who took thy hand and wooed thee as a lover" (A. V. xviii. 3. 1, 2). The second of the above mantras has been translated otherwise also:—"Go up, O woman, to the world of the living; thou liest by this one who is deceased: come! to him who grasps thy hand, thy second spouse, thou hast now entered into the relation of wife to husband:" This was possibly the earlier interpretation and the mantra was understood in this sense when the brother of the deceased took his wife; he then recited this mantra and grasped her hand and raised her from the funeral pile. The wife was led back to her home (A. V. xviii. 3. 3). A goat was then slaughtered and its parts laid on those of the corpse. Fire was applied to the funeral pile and women with dishevelled locks beat their breasts, shrieked and danced in wild grief round the funeral fire. The priest muttered a prayer to Agni. "Burn him not up; nor quite consume him; let not his body or his skin be scattered. O Jātavedas, when thou hast matured him then send him on his way unto the Fathers. . . . Thy portion is the goat: with heat consume him: let thy fierce flame, thy glowing splendour, burn him. With thine auspicious forms, O Jātavedas, bear this man to the region of the Fathers" (A. V. xviii. 2. 4, 8). In the case of the man who has given the v i s h ṭ a r i oblation, Jātavedas does not burn away his s i s' n a m during cremation and he will be enabled to meet "much women-folk." The various parts of the dead man's body were then directed to go to appropriate places. "The sun receive thine eye, the wind thy breath (ā t m ā); go according to thy nature to earth or heaven. Go, if it suits you, unto the waters; go, make thine home in plants with all thy members" (R. V. x. 16. 3). The bones were then collected and buried and in some cases a funeral monument was erected. "Heave thyself, Earth, nor press thee downward heavily: afford him easy access, gently tending him. Cover him, as a mother wraps her skirt about her child, O Earth. Now let the heaving earth be free from motion: yea, let a thousand clods remain above him. Be they to him a home distilling fatness, here let them ever be his place of refuge. I stay the earth from thee, while over thee I place this piece of earth. May I be free from injury. Here let the fathers keep this pillar (s t h ū ṇ a, of the funeral monument) firm for thee, and there let Yama make for thee an abiding-place" (R. V. x. 18 11—13). The man himself was bidden to "Go forth, go forth upon the ancient pathways whereon our sires of old have gone before us. . . . Meet Yama, meet the Fathers, meet the merit of free or ordered acts, in highest heaven. Leave sin and evil, seek anew thy dwelling and, bright with glory, wear another body" (R. V. x. 14. 7, 8). Cremation was the ordinary method of disposal of the dead among the followers of the fire-cult, but burial, casting away (p a r o p t a h) and exposing (u t t h i t a h) old men to die of hunger, as Praskanvas was, (R. V. v a l. 3. 2) are also mentioned (A. V. xviii. 2. 34).

On the completion of the funeral rites, the corpse-eating Agni (k r a v y ā d) which had been invoked for cremation had to be sent out of the house (A. V. xii. 2.4), as also G r ā h i "who holds fast in his net the house where a dame's husband dies" (A. V. xii. 2. 39). The people bathed, if possible in a river, to purge the pollution due to worshipping the funeral fire

(*Ib.* 40-42) and Jātavedas, the pure, sacrificial fire, was lighted and the gracious "tiger" (the sacrificial fire) was invoked to drive out the "ungracious one" (the funeral fire)', and to prolong the lives of the survivors (*Ib.* 43-45). A black ewe, lead and mashed beans were offered to the corpse-eating fire to induce him to desert the bed of the deceased person (*Ib.* 53). Sugar-cane and white sesamum were offered to Indra who finally removed the fire of Yama (*Ib.* 54). Then there was feasting and resumption of "dancing and laughter." (R. V. x. 18. 3). Thus all the four parts of the complete funeral rite, the burning, the asthi sañchayanam (the collection of bones and depositing them in urns), the s'ānti karmā (expiation), and the smas'āna chiti, (erection of monument) existed in old days.

At death the man was believed to be sundered into "three separate parts"; one was burnt and its remains buried to "sink downward" in the earth; another went "yonder", to the sun, the wind, etc. (A. V. xi. 8. 33). The third unborn (aja) part went further, beyond the first heaven which is watery (udanvatī), beyond the second heaven, starry, (pīlumatī), on to the third, the fore-heaven (pradyaus) in which the Fathers dwelt (A. V. xviii. 2. 48). Invested with a body of light (A. V. xi. 1. 37) he went in a car or on wings (A. V. iv. 34. 4), to the land of eternal light (R. V. ix. 113-7); fanned by delicious winds, cooled by showers, he recovered his complete form, body, mind and life (A. V. xviii. 2. 24), hastened past Yama's two four-eyed, broad-nosed, brindled, brown dogs, sons of Saramā, (R. V. x. 14. 10, 11) and reached the region where Yama dwells under the As'vattha tree (A. V. v. 4. 3), drinking with the gods (R. V. x. 135. 1), minstrels playing on the flute (nālī) and singing his praises (R. V. x. 135.7). This is the region of Vishnu's highest step (A. V. xviii. 1. 45, R. V. i. 155.5). There he joined the company of the Fathers and led a happy life reunited with father, mother, wives and children (A. V. vi. 120. 3, xii. 3. 6, 17). Life there is free from imperfections and all desires are fulfilled (R. V. ix. 113. 9, 11). His descendants still living in the world of men very often performed s'rāddham, invited him and other dead ancestors to sit southward on the sacred grass, partake of their favourite oblations and bless their offspring, still living in the mortal world, with treasure, energy, and a multitude of heroic sons (R. V. x. 15. 4—11). The mantras used in the s'rāddham were the same as those used in our days, though now s'raddham is regarded as a duty to the dead, and not as in old times, a method of securing their benediction. The Fathers were invoked with "Come hither Fathers, who deserve the Soma, by the deep pathways which the Fathers travel. Bestow upon us life and store of children, and favour us with increase of riches" (A. V. xviii. 4. 62). "May they ascend, the lowest, highest, midmost, the Fathers who deserve a share of Soma. May they who have attained the life of spirits, gentle and righteous, aid us when we call them" (R. V. x. 15. 1). "Our Fathers are Angirases, Navagvas, Atharvaṇas, Bhrigus, who deserve the Soma. May these, the Holy, look on us with favour, may we enjoy their gracious loving kindness." (R. V. x. 14. 6). Then the following prayers called madhutrayam, three passages beginning the word with madhu, sweet, were uttered. "Sweet the winds waft, sweet the rivers pour for the man who keeps the law; sweet may the plants be to us. Sweet be the night and sweet the dawns, sweet the terrestrial atmosphere; sweet be our Father heaven, to us. Sweets for us may the tall tree be full of, and full of sweets the sun. Sweet may our milch-kine be for us." (R. V. i. 90. 6-8). The Fathers were then asked to go back. "Depart, O Fathers, ye who merit Soma, by the deep pathways which the Fathers travel; but in a month, rich in fair sons and heroes, come back into our homes to eat oblation" (A. V. xviii. 4. 63). These ceremonies were performed on new-moon days.

Evil people went to hell (n a r a k a), the house down below (A. V. ii. 14. 3). There the man that has spat or shot his rheum upon a Brāhmaṇa, sat in the middle of a stream running with blood, devouring hair (*Ib.* V. 19. 3). It is the lowest darkness (*Ib.* 30. 11), the blind darkness (A. V. xviii. 3. 3), full of demons (A. V. ix. 2. 18) and y ā t u d h ā n ī s (female goblins, A. V. ii. 14. 3). Unchaste girls and unfaithful wives also went to hell (R. V. iv. 5. 5). So, too, the ignorant who did not sing the praises of the gods and join in sacrifices. (*Ib.* ix. 64. 21).

It will thus be seen that life in Ancient India, more than 3000 years ago was as complex, as much civilized, as it is to-day everywhere in India, in places unaffected by the railway and the telegraph and the amenities of western civilization. A brief account of the culture of the peoples among whom the Indo-Germanic dialects evolved before the dawn of history may serve to enable the reader to realize how much of this civilization of the people of Old India was Indian in origin and how little borrowed from the foreigners from whom North India derived the parent of its vernaculars. The original home of the Indo-Germanic language was the long stretch of grass-land extending from the north of the Carpathians and the Lower Danube to the foot-hills below Altai and Tianshan in Central Asia, skirting the shores of the Black Sea and the Caspian, and extending south to the Caucasus and the steep north edge of Persia. This was the area of characterization of a race of tall, fair-skinned, blue-eyed, narrow-headed giants to whom the name Proto-Nordics has been given. The grass-land made them develop a pastoral life, modified by some hunting on the one hand and some very primitive agriculture on the other. Their one notable contribution to the growth of the world's civilization was that they domesticated the horse ; the horse was first broken in to be ridden and later on to drag a wheeled vehicle for the transport of goods. Other domestic animals they had, the pig, the dog, the sheep, the goat and the cow. Periodical dessication of the grass-land made these people mobile and prefer a pastoral to an agricultural life. Like the modern Tartars they drove their herds with them and depended on their meat and milk for food and on their skins for clothing. Their social structure was patriarchal and their households lived in loosely federated groups. Their culture was not much above that of the stone age ; for the names for the smith did not grow up among the speakers of the Indo-Germanic dialects when they were ethnologically united, nor do the names of the tools in those dialects show the least trace of a common origin (Schrader : *Prehist. Antiq. Ar. Peoples*, pp. 158-159). There are only two words common to the Indo-Germanic languages, applied to metals, a y a s, and l o h a. A y a s corresponds to Ital. a e s, Goth. a i z, A. S ā r (Eng. o r e) and these words were originally used for raw copper as well as for bronze. Copper and bronze were in early days worked by the people that surrounded the great steppe-land where the Nordics roved—the Sumero-Accadians, the pure Semites, etc. The name a y a s originally referred to the bronze, tools made of which the grass-landers acquired in their wanderings. When Sanskrit reached India, this word was however transferred to iron, for India was then in the iron age and this metal had been named and worked in India before the arrival of this Indo-Germanic tongue. Similarly the word l o h a, Lat. r a u d u s, meaning red, first meant native copper, but in India, came to be also applied to iron, "a common process in the history of languages, *Cf.* Finn. v a s k i, copper, Hung. v a s, iron (*Ib.* pp 188—190). These steppe-landers ate animal food and drank an intoxicating liquor, called Sansk. m a d h u, Gr. m e t h u, O. H. Germ. m e t u, E. m e a d. "The meaning, 'honey,' which this series of words may take in numerous languages, and the idea of drunkenness [Sansk. m a d a, Gr. m e t h a, O. I. m e s c e = m e d c e] developed from it by these peoples, shows that we have here to do with an intoxicating drink of which the most essential constituent must have been honey" (*Ib* p. 321). They moved about in wagons, the root v e g h being found in all Indo-Germanic dialects; but the terms for spokes and felloes diverge, indicating that the wagons were furnished with primitive wheels without spokes. In the intervals of their wanderings, they lived in huts and houses, as is proved by the following linguistic equations: Sansk. d ā m a, Gr. d o m o s, Lat. d o m u s; Sansk. s' ā l ā, Gr. k a l i a, Lat. c e l l a, Teut. h a l l a. From similar linguistic considerations, we infer that the houses where these people lived were built of wood, basket-work and loam. (*Ib.* pp. 341-342). Private property in land was not known to them, though they had learnt to barter (*Cf.* Sansk. v a s n a, price, Lat. v e n-d o, Slav. v e n o, dowry). Herds of cattle formed the wealth of each household (*Cf.* Sansk. s' a r d h a = Goth. b a i r d a) and cattle was the standard of value (*Cf.* Sansk. p a s' u, Lat. p e c u s, Goth. f a i h u, Eng. f e e). These people did not bury their dead but burnt them. There is no common word for the sea in the Indo-Germanic languages, for they had never seen it.

About 2500 B.C., a great wave of dessication seems to have passed over Asia, which converted steppes into deserts and drove the great pastoral tribes of the steppes of the north as well as the Semites of the Arabian grass-land in search of pastures new. This great displacement of tribes included the "Canaanite" invasion of Syria, referred to in the *Genesis* and the Semite migration into Mesopotamia, leading to the establishment of a powerful Babylonian monarchy. From the northern steppes, the Nordics went out in many branches. One went by way of the Persian plateau into the interior of Asia Minor and on to Egypt, where they introduced the horse. Other branches settled both west and east of Babylonia and spread to the Mesopotamian valley, where, too, they introduced the horse; and when the Babylonians saw the horse, it was so strange to them that they named it, "the ass of the East." Another branch settled in Bactria and Eastern Iran. These movements profoundly affected the history of Asia; they cut off the jade and other trade between Khotan and Western Asia and deflected Babylonian trade to the Red Sea route. The branch that settled in Bactria dropped some of its nomadic habits and made some progress in agriculture, as is testified by the presence of y a v a in Sanskrit and in Zend, of Sansk. d h ā n ā, Zend. d ā n a, corn, Sansk. u r v a r ā, Zend. u r v a r a, field of crops, Sansk. s a s y a, Zend. h a h y a, seed-corn. for which undeniable counterparts are not found in the European languages (*Ib.* pp. 282—284). In this region, these people developed a taste for the soma-juice and primitive forms of the soma-cult and fire-cult were evolved here. They first met with gold, in this region, as Sansk. h i r a n y a corresponds with Zend. z a r a n y a; but they did not learn the work of the smith, as Sansk. d h m ā t ā is unconnected with the Zend. s a ə p a, melting-furnace. In this region the parent of the Vedic and Avestan languages underwent some phonetic changes also; then the proto-vedic tongue and simpler forms of the worship of fire and soma drifted to India from the Bactrian plateau, we do not know how. If the blonde giants of the North associated with Turki tribes of the plateau ever invaded India, it was so long before the composition of the Vedic hymns that there is no trace of a memory of such invasion in them. More probably it was a peaceful overflow of language and culture from the tableland to the plains. This occurred early enough for the foreign culture to mix intimately with the indigenous culture of the valleys of the Indus and the Ganges and for the fire-cult to develop in complexity as it did before the age of the Mantras.

The hymns of the Veda, too, are not the simple ballads of primitive pastoral tribes but bear marks of an antecedent literary culture of which they are the crowning product. The innumerable similes which are scattered through them and which, luckily, form the basis on which rest so many deductions regarding the life of the people given in the preceding pages indicate a long line of literary development on Indian soil. A few more specimens of the poetic imagery of the Rishis are transcribed below, to show the keen eye for nature the old Indian poets had cultivated. "As mother-mares run to their new-born youngling, so at his birth the gods wondered at Agni" (R. V. iii. 1. 4). Agni, "the unerring one, observant, found in floods, couched like a lion" (R. V. iii. 9. 4). "My heart quakes like a rolling wheel for fear of penury" (R. V v. 36. 3).

"These Maruts followed close, like lightning from the sky" (R. V. v. 52. 6). "At this liberal patron's rite they joy like cattle in the meadow" (R. V. v. 156). "Impetuous as a bear, O Maruts, is your rush, terrible as a dreadful bull" (R. V. v. 56. 3). "Like birds of air they flew with might in lengthened lines from heaven's high ridges to the borders of the sky" (A. V. v. 59. 7). "Advancing to be captured like a lion to the ambuscade" (R. V. v. 74. 4). "Like as the wind on every side ruffles a pool of lotuses, so stir in thee the babe unborn, so may the ten-month babe descend. Like as the wind, like as the wood, like as the sea is set astir, so, also, ten-month babe, descend" (R. V. v. 78. 7-8). "Like a rushing flood, loosed quickly, [Agni] burneth, swift as a guilty thief over desert places" (R. V. vi. 12. 5). "Strong, Lord [Indra], thine energies, endowed with vigour, are like the paths of kine converging homeward. Like bonds of cord, Indra, that bind the younglings, no bonds are they, O thou of boundless bounty" (R. V. vi. 24. 4). "By song and sacrifice men brought the waters from thee, as from a mountain's ridge, O Indra, urging thy might, with their fair lauds, they seek thee, O theme of song, as horses rush to battle" (R. V. vi. 24. 6). "These draughts come to thee, as milch-kine hasten to their young" (R. V. vi. 45. 28). "Thy teeth glance like lances' points within thy mouth when thou would bite" (R. V. vii. 55. 2). "The wind hath sounded through the region like a wild beast that seeks his food in pastures" (R. V. vii. 87. 2). "For me ten bright-hued oxen have come forward like lotus-stalks from out a lake upstanding" (R. V. xiii. 1. 33). "Flashing and whitely gleaming in her mightiness, she moves along her ample volumes through the realms, most active of the active, Sindhu, unrestrained, like to a dappled mare, beautiful, fair to see." (R. V. x. 75. 7).

The hymns to Ushas, the Dawn-maiden, reach a very high level of poetic excellence. "Like an active woman, Ushas advances cherishing all things; she hastens on, arousing footed-creatures, and makes the winged ones fly aloft. She sends forth the active and the beggars alike to their work; lively, she loves not to stand still; the flying birds no longer rest after thy dawning, O bringer of food. She hath yoked her horses from the remote rising place of the sun; this Ushas goes forth to men with a hundred chariots" (R. V. i. 48. 6-7). "The rosy beams have flashed up spontaneously; they have yoked the self-yoked ruddy cows. ......Like women, active in their work, they shine from afar along a common track; they bring food to the pious and liberal worshipper and all things to one who offers the juice of the soma. Ushas, like a dancer, puts on her gay attire; she displays her bosom as a cow its udder: creating light for all the world, she has scattered the darkness, as cattle go out of their stall" (R. V. i. 92. 2—4). "Like a maid triumphing in her beautiful form, thou, goddess, advancest to meet the god who seeks after thee; smiling, youthful and resplendent, thou unveilest thy bosom in front. Like a fair girl adorned by her mother thou displayest thy body to the beholder" (R. V. i. 123. 10-11). "She has been beheld like the bosom of a bright maiden. Like a poet, she has revealed things that we love. Awakening the sleepers like a fly, she has come, the most constant of women who have returned. As a woman who has no brother goes forth to meet a man, as a man with a chariot goes forth in pursuit of riches, as a loving wife shows herself to her husband, so does Ushas, as it were, smiling, reveal her form" (R. V. i. 124. 4, 7). "As conscious that her limbs are bright with bathing, she stands, as it were, erect that we may see her. Driving away malignity and darkness, Dawn, child of Heaven, hath come to us with lustre. The daughter of the sky, like some chaste woman, bends, opposite to men, her forehead downward. The maid, disclosing boons to him who worships, hath brought again the daylight, as aforetime" (R. V. v. 80. 5, 6).

The hymn to Araṇyānī, the forest maiden is also replete with beauty. "Araṇyānī, Araṇyānī, thou who seemest to vanish, why dost thou not go to the village? Does not terror seize thee? When the bull utters its roar, the chichichika bird replies, dancing, as if with cymbals; and then Araṇyānī rejoices. (In the evening twilight), the cows are dimly seen to be eating, houses are just discernible and Araṇyānī seems to send away her carts. One man calls to his cow, another fells a tree; a forest-dweller fancies that Araṇyān has screamed. Araṇyānī herself does not kill, if no one else, (a tiger or other wild beast) does not assail. Then a man after eating of sweet fruit, rests there at his pleasure. I laud Araṇyānī, the mother of wild beasts, sweet-smelling like balm, fragrant, who gives plenty of food, though no hinds till her" (R. V. x. 146).

As so very little of the Indian civilization of the age of the Mantras was derived from the speakers of the Indo-Germanic progenitor of the Vedic speech, very few of the gods of the Veda, too, were imported from without India. The numerous equations of Vedic gods with Greek, Lithuanian and other gods were due to a false method of inquiry which has been rightly condemned by Dr. Macdonnell. [1] "In the earlier period of Vedic studies there was a tendency to begin at the wrong end. The etymological equations of comparative mythology were then made the starting point." (*Ved. Myth.* p. 5). These equations have since been proved to be phonetically impossible, and the only god common to the speakers of the Vedic tongue and of Greek is D y a u s = Z e u s and the only conception common to Vedic and Greek mythology is the conception of Earth as a mother and Heaven as a father (D y a u s p i t a r = Z e u p ā t e r). This does not take us far, because the idea of Heaven and Earth being universal parents is common to so many people from China to Egypt, from Norway to New Zealand. Numerous other identifications, *e.g.*, Varuna with Ouranos, Ushas with Aurora have broken down under criticism. From the fact that the proto-Vedic and the proto-Avestandialects evidently grew side by side for some time on the Bactrian plateau since they left the original steppe-land home, a decided community of gods may be expected between Vedic and Avestan mythology but it is very surprising that the only god they have in common and that a minor god is Mitra, Mithra. All other Indian gods evolved in this country and apparently without any foreign influence.

Agni was the chief terrestrial deity of the "Arya." "The forehead of the sky, earth's centre, Agni became the messenger of earth and heaven. Vais'vānara, the deities produce thee, a god to be a light unto the Arya" (R. V. i. 59. 2). Indra generated him between two stones (*Ib.* ii. 12. 3) of old, as till recently he was produced in remote places in the jungle by striking flint on flint; but in the age of the Mantras he was produced by the churning of fire-sticks (a r a ṇ i). "Here is the a d h i m a n t h a n a m, the upper fire-stick with the string for whirling it; here is made ready the p r a j a n a n a m (the tuft of dried grass to propagate the flame); bring the v i s' p a t n ī (the mistress of the people, the lower piece of wood); we will rub Agni in the ancient fashion. In the two a r a ṇ i s Jātavedas lieth, even as the well-set germ in pregnant women, Agni who day by day must be exalted by men who watch and worship with oblations. Lay this (upper a r a ṇ i) with care on that (the lower) which lies extended. Being impregnated she speedily brings forth the vigorous one" (R. V. iii. 29. 1—3). The upper araṇi was made of a s v a t t h a and the lower of the s' a m ī and the production of fire is therefore compared to p u t r a s y a v e d a n a m (A. V. vi. 21. 1). The mystery of the production of fire from the fire-sticks and the apparent similarity of it to sexual reproduction profoundly affected the imagination of the Rishis. "He is produced from the two a r a ṇ i s as an infant newly-born" (R. V. v. 3. 9). The lower a r a ṇ i was called Urvas'ī and the upper Purūravas (S. Y. S. v. 2), and the commentator on this passage explains U r v a s'-y a s i thus: Y a t h ā U r v a s' ī p u r ū r a v o n r i-p a s y a b h o g ā y a a d h a s t ā t s' e t e t a d v a t t v a m a d h o v a s t h i t ā s i. Similarly the charm to ensure the birth of a boy runs, "The Asvattha [has] mounted upon the Samī; there is made the generation of a male" (A. V. vi. 11 1). The fire drill of the Indian rite has been taken by some as corresponding to the Prometheus of Greek mythology but this identification has proved to be false. "P r a m a n t h a, the name of this [upright] fire-drill, occurring for the first time in a late metrical Smriti work, the K a r m a p r a d ī p a (i. 7. 5) has, owing to a superficial resemblance, been connected with Prometheus." This is one of the fanciful equations of comparative mythology which later research has proved to be baseless. "The latter word has, however, every appearance of being purely a Greek formation, while the Indian verb m a t h, to twirl, [probably a root borrowed from Dravidian sources], is found compounded only with n i s, never with pra, to express the act of producing fire by friction." (Macdonnel, *Ved. Myth.* p. 91). Hence the Indian fire-cult and the Greek story of Prometheus stealing fire out of heaven have nothing to do with each other. The chief reason for choosing Agni, the wonder-worker (A. V. xviii. 1. 21) as the tongue of the gods (R. V. ii. 1. 13), their oblation-bearer (R. V. x. 46. 10), the invoker and herald who brings the gods to the sacrificial hall and seats them on the grass (R. V. iii. 14. 2; i. 13. 7), was that the Rishis were profoundly impressed with the sight of the fire-god "eating the woods" (R. V. i. 65. 4), both when it was spontaneously produced in the rich forests of the Indo-Gangetic valley and when it was lighted by men to clear forest-ground. "Like one athirst, he lighteth up forests; like water down the chariotways he roareth. On his black path he shines in burning beauty, marked as it were the heaven that shines through vapour. Around, consuming the broad earth, he wanders free, roaming like an ox without a herdsman, Agni refulgent burning up the bushes, with blackened lines, as though the earth he seasoned" (R. V. ii. 4. 6, 7). "Urged by the wind he spreads through dry wood as he lists, armed with his tongues for sickles, with a mighty roar. Black is thy path, Agni, changeless, with glittering waves, when like a bull thou rushest eager to the trees. With teeth of flame, wind-driven, through the wood he speeds, triumphant like a bull among the herd of cows, with bright strength to the ever-lasting air; things fixed, things moving, quake before him as he flies" (R. V. i. 58. 4, 5). Another use of Agni was to help to kill demons (R. V. x. 87. 1) or to drive them away (R. V. iii. 15. 1). The Vājasaneya Samhitā distinguishes three kinds of Agni, the āmād, eater of raw flesh, the kravyād, the eater of corpses, and the devayaja, fit for sacrificing to the gods (i. 17). The Taittirīya Samhitā also distinguishes three, (ii. 5. 8. 6), the havyavāhana, bearer of oblations to the Gods, invoked with the mystical call svāhā, the kavyavāhana, bearer of funeral oblations to the Fathers, invoked with svadhā and the saharakshas, associated with goblins and belonging to the Asuras. The sacrificial fire, Vais'vānara, has three places (yoni) in the sacrificial hall (R. V. ii. 36. 4), the gārhapatya, domestic, the āhavanīya, eastern, for receiving oblations and the dakshiṇa, southern, the three representing the terrestrial fire (R. V. i. 59. 2); besides, there was the fire of the ærial waters in lightning (R. V. vi. 6. 2) and the celestial fire, the sun (R. V. iii. 2. 14). A fire-cult of some form or other existed in old days among the Chaldeans, the Persians, the Greeks, the Italians, the Semites, etc., and burnt offerings were given to the gods bv all the nations of antiquity. But the Indian fire-cult has peculiar characteristics which indicates its special development in India, independent of foreign influence. Among no other people was the fire-god so definitely anthropomorphized and nor did he anywhere else acquire such a distinct individuality and such active duties. The Indian fire-god has a head (R. V. vii. 3. 1), a face (R. V. iii. 1. 18), tongues (R. V. iii. 6. 2), hairs (R. V. viii. 49. 2), a beard (R. V. v. 7. 7), thousand eyes (R. V. i. 79. 12), thousand horns (R. V. vi. 1. 8), and sahasramushka (R. V. viii. 19. 32). He chews the forest with sharp teeth (R. V. i. 143. 5), and eats it with his burning jaws (R. V. i. 58. 5). He rushes through the wood armed with tongues for sickles (R. V. i. 58. 4) and shaves the earth as a barber a beard (R. V. x. 142. 4). He is a king who goes with his attendants, spreading nets to catch birds and then shoots them with burning darts (R. V. iv. 4 1). "Fierce is his gait and vast his wondrous body; he champeth like a horse with bit and bridle, and darting forth his tongue, as it were a hatchet, burning the woods, smelteth them like a smelter. Archer-like, fain to shoot, he sets his arrow, and whets his splendour like the edge of iron. The messenger of night with brilliant pathway, like a tree-roosting bird of rapid pinion" (R. V. vi. 3. 4, 5). Though the mouth and the tongue with which the gods eat the sacrificial offering (R. V. ii. 1. 13, 14), and a messenger (d ū t a) of the gods, (R. V. i. 72. 7) who brings them to the sacrifice (R. V. iii. 14. 2), as well as takes it to them (R. v. vii. 11. 5), he is yet a high god and exercises the highest divine functions. He is the divine monarch (s a m r ā j o a s u r a s y a, R. V. vii. 6. 1), who spread out the two worlds like two skins (R. V. vi. 8. 3) ; he is the j ā t a v e d a s, a title peculiar to him and applied to him about 120 times, for he knows the birth of all. He is the Sun (R. V. iii. 2. 14), he is Indra, Vishṇu, Varuṇa, Mitra and most other gods, he is Aditi and other goddesses (R. V. ii. 1.). He is the germ (g a r b h a) of waters, of woods, of all that move not and all that move (R. V. i. 70. 2.). From all this it is evident that the Indian Agni has as little in common with the fire-gods of other countries as the elaborate Indian fire-worship with those of other ancient nations. Though the idea of offering sacrifices through fire was unknown to the Indian before the arrival of the proto-Vedic tongue and associated customs into Iṇdia, yet there is ample evidence in the Mantras to prove that the Indian method of fire-worship was developed in India and under the guidance of Indian priests. "Manu has placed thee (here) a light to all (generations of) men" (R. V. i. 36. 19). "Like Bhrigu, like Manush, like

Angiras, we invoke thee who hast been summoned to blaze" (R. V. viii. 43. 13). "Agni, Atharvā drew thee forth from the lotus leaf. Thee, Dadhyak, the son of Atharvā, kindled" (R. V. vi. 16. 13, 14). "The Bhrigus have placed thee among men" (R. V. i. 58. 6). And as if to accentuate the contrast between the Indian fire-god into whose mouth animal offerings were thrown and the fire-god of the Zoroastrians, jealously guarded from such pollution, the latter called him Ātar and gave up the Indo-European word Agni (Lat. i g n i s, Slav. o g n i).

Indra was the favourite god of the Indians of the age of the Mantras. He is praised in more hymns, and is referred to more often, than other gods. His special weapon is the thunderbolt (v a j r a) with which he smites the demons of drought, typed by Vritra (R. V. i. 80. 11, etc.) and lets loose the streams held by the clouds (R. V. iv. 19. 8, etc.) He creates the lightnings of heaven (R. V. ii. 13. 7) and directs the waters downwards (R. V. ii. 17. 3). He is also the great god of battle invoked by heroes in battles (R. V. iv. 24. 3, etc.). He is the ocean of riches (R. V. i. 51. 1) and all the paths of riches lead to him as the rivers to the sea (R. V. vi. 19. 5). His capacity for drinking Soma was enormous; he drank thirty bowls at one draught (R. V. viii. 66. 4); he was besides s a h a s r a m u s h k a (R. V. vi. 46. 3) and as said in a Brāhmaṇa legend, b h o g a l o l u p a t a y ā s v a s′ a r ī r e p a r v a ṇ i p a r v a ṇ i s′ e p ā n s a s r i j j a. Great god as he was, an Asura woman of the name of Vilistengā drew Indra from his place among the gods by means of her spells (A. V. vii. 38. 2). He then lived in the Asura world taking the form of a female when among females and of a male among males. Indra, like other gods, was human not only in qualities but also in form. His image was constructed in the Sautrāmaṇi rite, a cermony invented to cure Indra from the consquences of over-indulgence in Soma, with the following mantras: "This his immortal shape with mighty powers three Deities [the As'vins and Sarasvatī] bestowing gifts compounded. His hair they made with sprouts of grass and barley, and roasted grain with skin and flesh supplied him. His inner shape Sarasvatī arranges and, borne on bright paths, the physician As'vins. With m ā s a r a s [a mixture of boiled millet and surā] and sieve his bone and marrow, as on the oxen's hide they lay the liquor. By thought Sarasvatī with both Nāsatyas forms lovely treasure and a beauteous body. Like shuttle through the loom the steady ferment (n a g n a h u) mixed the red juice with the foaming spirit. By milk they generated bright immortal, productive seed, by s u r ā seed from wine, chasing after folly and ill-intention, crude food and wind and meat that loads the stomach. Heart with his heart Indra good guardian gendered; with rice-cake Savitā gave truth its being. Varuṇa doctoring the lungs and liver, forms as with vāyu cups, the gall and kidneys. Cooking pots pouring honey were the entrails; like a well-milking cow the pans were bowels. A hawk's wing was the spleen: through mighty powers the stool as mother was navel and belly. The pitcher was the father of the rectum by powers, the womb which first contained the infant. Plain was the hundred-streaming fount as p l ā s' i (s' i s' n a) the jar poured forth libations to the Father. His face the basket, thence his head; the strainer his tongue, his mouth Sarasvatī and As'vins. The c h a p y a (a vessel) was his rump, his leech the filter, the bladder was his s' e p a keen with ardour. As'vins with both cups made his eye immortal, the goat and cooked oblation gave it keenness. With wheat eyelashes and with jujube eye-brows they clothe as it were a black and brilliant figure. The sheep, the ram to give his nostril vigour, the immortal path of breath by both libations. By Indra-grains and sacrificial jujubes Sarasvatī produced thought-breath and nose-hairs. The bull for strength made Indra's form : the immortal hearing for both his ears by two libations. Barley and sacred grass composed his eyebrows : from his mouth came the jujube and sweet honey. Hair of the wolf was on his waist and body : the beard upon his face was hair of tigers. Lion's hair were his locks, for fame and beauty, worn on his head, his crest and sheen and vigour. The As'vins, leeches, joined his limbs and body, Sarasvatī put limbs and frame together giving the form and vital power of Indra, hundred-fold, deathless and delightful lustre" (S. Y. S. xix. 81—93). It has been remarked by some scholars that idolatry did not exist in the Vedic age, but there is little to distinguish the above from modern Hindu idolatry.

The conception of Indra held by the Rishis was so intensely anthropomorphic that it is difficult to discover whether in addition to his divine characteristics, he was also endowed by the Rishis with attributes possessed by historical personages. Some at least of Indra's exploits in releasing water seem to point to disputes about rights to river-water for irrigation purposes between his worshippers and men of other tribes who probably worshipped the snake and are referred to as the dragon. "Indra, the mighty one, the dragon's slayer, sent forth the flood of waters to the ocean (R. V. ii. 19. 3) "Floods great and many, compassed by the dragon, thou badest swell and settest free, O Hero" (R. V. ii. 11. 2.) "He slew the dragon lying on the mountain...Like lowing kine in rapid flow descending, the waters glided downward to the ocean." (R. V. i. 32. 2). "From front, as it were a house, he ruled and measured; dug out with his bolts channels for the streams" (R. V. ii. 15. 3). "He loosened the rock that the Brāhmaṇas easily found the cows (rivers)" (R. V. x. 112. 8). These and similar passages seem to refer to breaking open rocky dams and cutting channels and not to breaking the head of the drought demons and pirecing the clouds, to the bursting asunder solid (and not ærial) blocks and releasing the imprisoned water; in some at least of the references, human kings named after the God may be meant. Battles for the control of water-courses are frequently referred to. "What time the men in fury rush together for running streams, for pastures and for houses, then, O ye Maruts,...be our protection in the strife with foemen" (R. V. vii. 57. 22). "Who are the men whom thou wilt further, Indra, who strive to win thy bliss allied with riches? Who urged thee forward to exert thy power dīvine, to valour, in the war for waters on their fields?" (R. V. x. 50. 3). Similarly Vritra, whom Indra slew with his thunderbolt was no doubt the demon that imprisoned waters in the cloud, but the Vritras sometimes seem to refer to human tribes and not demons, as in "Auspicious Indra, best hero in the fight where spoil is gathered, the strong who listens, who gives aid in battles, who slays the Vritras, wins and gathers riches" (R. V. x. 89. 18). "Then wast thou, chieftain of all living mortals, the very mighty slayer of the Vritras; then didst thou set the obstructed rivers flowing, and with the floods that were enthralled by Dāsas" (R. V. viii. 85. 18). "Thou art king; alone thou smitest Vritras dead, to gain, O Indra, spoils of war and high renown" (R. V. viii. 15. 3). Indra's attempt to capture the cows of the Panis (R. V. x. 108) seems to refer to fights with a tribe of traders living near an actual river Rasā who refused to present priests of the fire-cult with cattle and not to meteorological phenomena. Many demons opposed to Indra, S'ambara, S'ushna, Pipru and others, were probably actual kings or perhaps gods of the tribes who refused to accept the worship of Indra. This worship, like the Agni cult, was elaborated in India. There are many hints in the Mantras which lead us to think that Indra rose to prominence in the age of the Mantras after a severe competition with other gods and that his cult eclipsed other cults. There are legends about Indra coming into conflict with the sun (R. V. x. 92. 8), with Varuṇa (R. V. iv. 42), with the Maruts (R. V. i. 170, 171), with the gods generally (R. V. iv. 30. 3, viii. 51. 7) and to have prevailed over the earlier deities (vii. 21. 7). To the same conclusion also point the legends of his birth (R. V. iii. 48; iv. 18). The etymology of his name is not known, though many wild guesses have been hazarded on the question by various people from the ancient Rishis down to modern scholars. His name, too, occurs but twice in the Avesta' in the form of Añdra, as that of a minor demon and that not in the earlier *Gāthas* but in the later *Vendidad* and even there, the passage where it occurs is omitted in two of the oldest manuscripts (Haug. *Essays on the Parsis*, p. 272). These facts clearly point to the conclusion that Indra was an Indian god who was not known on the Bactrian plateau and came to be known to the writers of the *Vendidad* as a foreign god to whom no great honour was due. The theory that the separation of the speakers of the Vedic and the Zend dialects was due to the acceptance by the former of Indra as the chief god has no shred of evidence to support it. Possibly future research will discover the root from which the name Indra is derived and it will perhaps prove to be a Dravidian root.

In a series of passages Indra is spoken of as wandering far. "From near or far away may mighty Indra come," (R. V. iv. 20. 1). "Hither let Indra come, from firmament or ocean;......or from a distance from the seat of Order" (R. V. iv. 21. 3). "Bearing a name renowned in far-off regions" (R. V. v. 30. 5). "Where is that Indra? Among what tribes? What people does he visit? What sacrifice contents thy mind and wishes? What priest among them all? What hymn, O Indra? Yea, here were they, who, born of old, have served thee, thy friends of ancient time, thou active worker. Bethink thee now of these, invoked of many" (R. V. vi. 21. 4-5). "Thou distant Roamer" (R. V. vi. 31. 5). "Who cometh nigh even from a distance" (R. V. vi. 38. 2). "Where art thou? Whither art thou gone? For many a place attracts thy mind" (R. V. viii. 1. 7). "Where is famed Indra heard of? With what folk is he renowned to-day as Mitra is?" (R. V. x. 22. 1). Let none delay thee far from us. Even from far away come thou unto our feast" (R. V. vii. 32. 1). Whither are ye gone? Whither, like falcons have ye flown?" (R. V. viii. 62. 4). "Though he is far away, we call to succour us" (R. V. viii. 75. 4). Indra was a god of the middle regions and Vishṇu of the highest regions; yet the latter is never said to wander far. Hence these passages suggest that the Indra-cult wandered to distant countries after its development in India. The implications of these passages will be discussed below in connection with the wanderings of the As'vīns.

Besides Indra and Agni, there were many other gods in the Vedic pantheon, but very few of them were non-Indian in origin. We have seen that only one, Dyaus, had his linguistic analogue among the European Indo-Germanic dialects. But the divine nature of Dyaus in the Mantras is so shadowy and his physical nature so predominant that we can scarcely infer that the Rishis imagined him as a god at all. There is only one god common to the Veda and the Avesta, though the dialects in which these scriptures are written are so nearly allied that whole passages of one can be translated into the other by the mechanical process of the substitution of word for allied word; and this god, Mitra, is a minor one in both mythologies. This proves either that the pastoral tribes from whom these dialects were derived did not possess a rich mythology or that the tribes of Persia and India that borrowed these languages did not take over the gods but evolved their own gods. Or perhaps the spread of these languages synchronized with a coalition of various tribes and the consequent growth of polytribal polytheism from tribal monotheism, such as occurred in Ancient Egypt. Recently an inscription was discovered at Baghaz-Keui in which Varuṇa, Mitra, Indra and the Nāsatya are invoked under the forms u r u w̥ n a, m i i t r a, i n d a r, n a s a a t t i i a, as witnesses to a treaty by a chief of the Mittani, who ruled the district near the western bend of the Euphrates in the XV Century B. C. The names of some of these chiefs look Indian—Artatama, Sutarna, Dushratta. This was certainly due to the wandering of the Indian gods, in the wake probably of an Indian prince or princess. Some scholars think that the document belongs to an age preceding that of the rise of Indian and Iranian mythology, but this cannot be because if Nāsatya and Varuṇa existed before the age of the Avesta, they could not have so completely dropped out of it. Indra, too, would not have become such an obscure demon. Moreover in the Mantras of the Rig Veda, there are several references to far-off places to which the Nāsatyas and Indra had wandered

"What make ye there, ye mighty [Nāsatyas]? Wherefore linger ye with folk who offering not are held in high esteem? Pass over them" (R. V. i. 182. 3). "Nāsatyas, wherever ye be, (we invoke ye)" (R. V. i. 184. 1). "Even through many regions, O ye As'vins, high praise is yours among mankind" (R. V. iii. 58. 5). "Whether, O As'vins, ye this day be far remote or near at hand" (R. V. v, 73. 1). "Traversing many wide unmeasured spaces, over the wastes ye pass, and fields and waters" (R. V. vi. 62. 2). "Come thou from the east, come from the west, Nāsatyas, come" (R. V. vii. 72. 5). "From far away ye come to us, As'vins, enjoying plenteous food of Dāsas" (R. V. viii. 5. 31). "Nāsatyas, whether ye be nigh or whether ye be far away, come thence" (R. V. viii. 8. 14.) "Nāsatyas, near or far away" (R. V. viii. 9. 15). "Whether ye, Lords of ample wealth, now linger in the east or west" (R. V. viii. 10. 5). "O As'vins, where and with what folk do you delight yourselves to-day" (R. V. x. 40. 14). The wandering of Indra to far-off countries has already been proved by a number of quotations. But one passage not quoted in the last paragraph throws light on this discussion. "O Indra, if you are regaling yourself in Ruma, Rus'ama, S'yavaka, Kripa, come" (R. V. viii. 4. 2). Ruma occurs also in the Avesta and is taken by scholars refer to Western Asia. This passage distinctly proves that the Indra-cult travelled to distant countries after its growth in India. It is also significant that Nāsatya occurs in the Mitani document as Na-*s*a-at-ti-ia, whereas the Avestan form of it is supposed by Spiegel (*Avesta* III. p. lxxxi. q. Muir. v. 121) to be Nāoghaithya. This again proves that Nāsatya went to Mitani straight from India without the intervention of the Persians. If the interpretation here given to these Mantras is not unreasonable, these hymns which refer to the wanderings of Indra and the As'vins must have been composed in the XV Century B.C.; if so the age of the Mantras commenced about the XVII Century B.C., which is surely not an extravagant claim. And if A. V. xix. 68 and 72, already quoted, refer to the Veda as a written book, as has been maintained above and as has been taken by Bloomfield, the latest mantras were composed about 1000 B.C., the time when writing was introduced into India. Two or three centuries before this, the composition of the Mantras practically ceased and none but the most modern of Mantras were composed after 1200 B.C. This conclusion is supported by the much-discussed passage referred to in the *Vedānga Jyotisha*, which mentions the tradition that the sun and the moon turned north and south respectively in the months of Māgha and S'rāvaṅa; this refers to the XII Century B.C., by which time the bulk of the Mantras were in existence.

All other Vedic gods, (1) Savitā, Pūshā, Vāyu, Sūrya, Ushas, the Maruts, Soma and Yama, (2) Varuṅa, Rudra, Tvashṭā and Aditi, (3) Brihaspati, Prajāpati, Skambha and Bramhaṅaspati are all purely Indian deities. Of these, the first group seems to have been evolved from germs of ideas brought along the current of the Indo-Germanic dialect that evolved into the language of the Mantras. The etymology of most of these names is plain, but deities corresponding to them in name and function are not found outside India. The gods of the second group seem to have been taken over from the Dravidian-speaking tribes of India. It has been already pointed out that the Dravidian languages profoundly affected the Vedic language. Similarly the gods worshipped by the tribes that gradually accepted this language must have been "aryanized" and adopted into the Vedic pantheon. Those Vedic gods the etymology of whose names is not patent and who have no analogues in other Indo-Germanic dialects must have been Indian gods to whom such treatment was accorded. The first of these seems to have been Varuṇa. He was once identified by scholars with the Greek Ouranos and believed to be a sky god, but this identification has now been abandoned on account of phonetic difficulties. Under the influence of this identification, scholars have without any proof thought that Varuṇa was at first a god of the sky, then became the god of the ærial ocean and lastly of the water ocean. This theory based entirely on *a priori* considerations, is both against Indian tradition and the evidence of the Rig Veda. The connection of Varuṇa with water is referred to in numerous Mantras. "He made them flow, the Āditya, the sustainer: the rivers run by Vàruṇa's commandment" (R. V. ii. 28. 4). Varuṇa and Mitra are called "Lords of Rivers" in R. V. vii. 64. 2. But Varuṇa's being the sea-god is explicitly referred to in various Mantras. "Varuṇa comes in the sea's gathered waters, O sons of strength, desirous of your presence" (R. V̄. i. 161. 14). "None, verily, hath ever let or hindered this, the most wise God's mighty deed of magic, whereby with all their flood, the lucid rivers fill not one sea wherein they pour their waters" (R. V. v. 85. 6). "Mitra and Varuṇa, ye two kings, protectors of the great ceremonial, strong lords of the sea, come hither" (R. V. vii. 64. 2). "Like Varuṇa, from heaven he [the sun] sinks in the sea, like a white-shining spark" (R. V. vii. 87. 6). "Thou art a glorious god, into whose jaws the seven rivers flow, as into a surging abyss." (R. V. viii. 58. 12). "Soma lives in the woods as Varuṇa in the sea" R. V. ix. 90. 2). "Varuṇa, the child of the waters, made his abode within the most motherly waters as in his home" (S. Y. S. x. 7). "The two oceans are Varuṇa's stomachs" (A. V. iv. 16. 3). "Thy golden house, Varuṇa, is in the waters" (A. V. vii. 83. 1). The waters are the wives of Varuṇa (T. S. v. 5. 4. 1). The references to the ocean are few in the Vedic Mantras, because their authors lived inland; hence the comparative rareness of references to Varuṇa, who according to the statistical standard is but a third class deity. Probably Varuṇa was the God of the tribes living on the borders of the sea, to whom the Rishis accorded a place in their pantheon. The etymology of the name is obscure.

Rudra seems to have been another god of the Dravidian-speaking tribes. He is essentially a mountain deity (S. Y. S. xvi 2, 4) wearing braided hair (R. V. i. 114. 1, 5); his colour is brown (b a b h r u, R. V. ii. 33. 5), red (S. Y. S. xvi. 7) and he is clothed in skin (S. Y. S. iii. 61). He is an archer (A. V. i. 28. 1, etc.), fierce (R. V. ii. 33, 10) destructive like a terrible beast (R. V. ii. 33. 11), a malevolent destroyer (R. V. ii. 33. 11, 14), man-slaying (R. V. iv. 3. 6), followed by wide-mouthed howling dogs, who swallow their prey unchewed (A. V. xi. 2. 30). He was "lord of the green-haired trees," who "glides away" and whom cowherds and female drawers of water have seen; he was lord of thieves, carpenters, chariot-makers, potters, blacksmiths, Nishādas, dog-leaders and hunters (S. Y. S. xvi.). Such a deity could be evolved by the wild mountaineers of the Himalayan or Vindhyan regions and not by the mild Rishis of the valleys. His name, too, Rudra meaning the Red One seems to be a translation of the Dravidian name S'iva (which is the Dravidian word for 'red') later on adopted for the same god. Tvashṭā was probably the god of artificers, who was supplanted by Indra (R. V. iii. 48. 4). The antecedents of Aditi whose name has baffled ancient as well as modern etymologers cannot be discovered. Vishṇu's name is popularly derived from v i s h, to pervade, but the Vedic Vishṇu was anything but a pervader. He dwelt in the highest heaven wherefrom he strode wide. He is a dweller of the mountains, terrible like a wild beast (R. V. i. 154). But his place is the highest station (R. V. iii. 55. 10) where there is a well of mead and where pious men rejoice (R. V. i. 154. 5) as well as the gods (R, V. viii. 29. 7). His name is probably derived from the Dravidian root v i ṇ, the sky, for he is essentially the sky-god. Vishṇu, S'iva and the mother (originally Aditi, later on, called by other names) are now the chief divinities of the Indians and this can be easily explained only if they were popular gods even before the Vedas were composed. To the Rishis they were minor gods, grudgingly admitted into their pantheon; but the people worshipped them, so that when the glory of the fire-cult was eclipsed, these gods again came by their rights. Besides these two classes of gods, the Rishis evolved many other gods out of abstractions; some of these were clothed with flesh, *e.g.*, Brihaspati, Prajāpati, Kāma, Vāk, but other remained abstractions, *e.g.*, Manyu, Arāti, S'raddhā and died out a natural death.

The study of the growth of religion in ancient Chaldea and ancient Egypt, has brought out the fact that among ancient people, religion progressed from tribal monotheism to inter-tribal polytheism; when tribes mingled, their gods, too, mingled; and as each tribe rose to prominence, its god became superior to the gods of other tribes. Something similar occurred too in ancient India. All the forty and odd tribes did not worship Indra as the chief god, as the Rig Veda Mantras themselves admit. Indra was the god of the tribes that rose to great power during this age and that produced a literature. This explains the so-called "henotheism" of the Vedas, referred to by Max Müller, in which each god, when lauded, is spoken of as superior to all other gods; this was because to some tribe or other, he was the chief god. This also explains why there are so many sun-gods—Sūrya, Savitā, Vishṇu, Mitra; so many atmospheric gods—Indra, Ribhus, Maruts, As'vins, etc. But as philosophic thought grew, the many gods were reduced to one and inter-tribal polytheism gave way to universal pantheism.

Besides these anthropomosphic gods, the people had many others, animistic and totemistic. The Vedas being manuals of the fire-cult, references to other cults can be but casual. Yet, we find in them a hymn addressed to the waters, part of which is repeated to-day by certain sections of Brāhmaṇas in their daily prayers. "Ye waters, are beneficent, so help ye us to energy that we may look on with great delight. Give us a portion of the sap, the most auspicious that ye have, like mothers in their longing love. To you we gladly come from him to whose abode ye send us on; and waters, give us procreant strength" (R. V. x. 9. 1—3). The virtues of Araṇyānī, the goddess of the wood, who wore a "green robe of trees" (A. V. x. 8. 31) are lauded in a hymn (R. V. x. 146). The holiness of the Asvattha, a tree frequently associated with the gods (R. V. i. 135. 8; A. V. v. 4. 3, etc.) and worshipped to-day for its property of stimulating the fecundity of woman and also used for making the fire-drill, symbol of the S'īs'na, has come down from the days when it was the totem of an ancient tribe. The Atharva Veda Samhitā contains a serpent hymn (A. V. iii. 26) and Ahi Budhnya was a serpent-god. Besides the celestial horses that dragged the cars of the gods and were therefore praised by the Rishis, individual horses were paid divine honours on their own account. Dadhikra was the chief of them (R. V. iv. 38, 39, 40; vii. 44). The cow was also held sacred and worshipped (A. V. xii. 4. 5). She is called by the name a g h n y a, not to be killed, in sixteen passages and curses are invoked on the person that killed a cow, especially one belonging to a Brāhmaṇa (A. V. xii. 4. 38). On account of reverence for the cow and possibly on account of economic causes also there arose before the end of this age a prejudice against eating beef which has gathered volume through the ages and is now become one of the characteristic marks of the members of the four Hindu castes.

Many of the demons with whom Indra fought were probably the gods of the tribes opposed to the Indra-worshippers. The chief of them was Vṛitra, called in various places an a h i, or serpent. Vṛitra was the god of a tribe called the Vṛitras, who were at constant enmity with the worshippers of Indra (R. V. vi. 33. 2; vi. 29. 6, etc.) Allied to the Vṛitras were the Paṇis, who worshipped Vala. Vṛitra lived on the mountains viii. 3. 19) and Vala in caves (R. V. i. 11. 5). The Paṇis were traders and had, "hoarded wealth and cattle" "wealth in horses and in kine" (R. V. i. 83. 4). They would not accept the fire-cult, though apparently a peaceful attempt was made to convert them. R. V. x. 108 is a dialogue between Saramā, the messenger of Indra and the Paṇis, in which Saramā invites the Paṇis to worship Indra "I know him safe from harm; but he can punish, who sent me hither from afar as envoy......how will you lie, O Paṇis, slain by Indra." The Paṇis gently reminded her that their "warlike weapons were also sharp-pointed." Saramā then told them that the Brāhmaṇas could wound them with their "words." But the Paṇis were proof against these arguments and hence execrated by the Rishis as niggards (R. V. x. 60. 6, etc.) In this connection it mus also be pointed out that the Turvasas, Yadus, Aṇus, Druhyus and Purus, usually taken by Vedic scholars to be the "five" "Arya" tribes mentioned in the Vedas were, according to the Puranic legends, sons of Yayāti whose two wives were both from the Asuras. Yayāti was the son of Nahusha, a rival of Indra, who became a serpent, being cursed by the Rishis. The Nahushas are described in R. V. vii. 6 as foolish, faithless, rudely speaking niggards and enemies of the fire-cult and in R. V. x. 49. 8, Indra is said to have defeated Nahusha. This shows that these were tribes of serpent-worshippers and foes of the Indra-Agni cult. The worship of the serpent is practically universal in modern India; and in the legends of the M a h a- b h ā r a t a and the Buddhist J ā t a k a tales the Nāgas are very prominent tribes; hence the serpent-cult must have been very widespread among the ancient Dravidian speaking people. The s' i s' n a, symbol of generation, as the serpent was of destruction, was also widely worshipped by these races and the two cults were allied to each other and referred together. "Thou heroic Indra has caused to flow the abundant waters which had been obstructed by the serpent (Ahi). Through thee the cows (rivers) have rolled on like warriors in chariots. All created things tremble for fear. The terrible (god), skilled in all heroic deeds, has with his weapons mastered these. Indra, exulting, has shattered their cities; armed with the thunderbolt, he has smitten them asunder by his might. Neither demons impel us, Indra, nor, O puissant, of a truth any evil spirits. The glorious [Indra], defies the hostile beings: let not those S i s' n a d e v a s approach our sacred ceremony. Thou, O Indra, hast surpassed in power, when thou runnest thy course. The worlds have not comprehended within them thy greatness. By thine own might thou hast slain Vritra. No enemy hath attained the end of thee in battle. The earlier gods have yielded to thy divine power; their powers have yielded to thy divine power; their powers have bowed before thy sovereign might. Indra having conquered dispenses wealth. Let men invoke Indra in the combat" (R. V. vii. 21. 3—7). This clearly proves that though in many passages Vritra and Indra refer to the drought demon and the god who with the thunderbolt bursts the clouds, originally they were gods of rival tribes and the tribes that worshipped Vritra, the serpent-god, either also worshipped or were associated with those that worshipped the S'isna also. There is another reference to those whose god is the s'is'na. "Proceeding to the conflict, and desiring to acquire them, he has gone to, and in hostile array besieged, inaccessible places, at the time, when, irresistible, slaying the S'is'na devas, he by his craft conquered the riches of the city with a hundred gates." (R. V. x. 99. 3) Sāyana's interpretation of S'is'na deva as one who sports with the S'is'na is clearly impossible, since the Rishis sported with the s'is'na quite as much as others (R. V. i. 126. 6, 7, 179, A. V. xx. 136, etc.) The S'ivas are mentioned as one of the tribes opposed to the Indra-worshipping Tritsus (R. V. vii. 18. 7), and the S'is'nas are referred to as advancing against Indra (R. V. x. 27. 19). Considering along with these the fact that the phallus-emblem of S'iva is even to-day inseparably bound up with his worship so widespread, the conclusion is irresistible that phallic worship was universal in ancient India and that the Indra-cult failed to displace the S'is'na-cult. On the contrary, the Rishis adopted the phallic worship, though not as a part of their fire-cult. One famous hymn, that to Skambha (A. V. x. 7) is a glorification of the divine phallus. "In what member of his does tapas stand? in what member is ritam contained? In what do vratam and s'raddhā reside? In what member is truth established? From what member does Agni blaze?......How far did Skambha penetrate into that highest, lowest, and middle universe?...How much of it was there which he did not penetrate?...Where Skambha generating, brought the ancient one into existence, they consider that that ancient one is one member of Skambha...Skambha in the beginning shed that gold (of which Hiraṇyagarbha arose) in the midst of the world...He who knows the golden phallus standing in the waters, he is the secret Prajāpati." Skambha is a phonetic variant of stambha, pillar, and is no other than the pillar of fire, the luminous phallus, "encircled with a thousand wreaths of flame," in which form S'iva appeared to Vishṇu and Brahma, as described in the *Linga Purāṇam* i. 17. For in A. V. x. 8, it is said that he who knows the two pieces of firewood, from which wealth is rubbed out will know the great divine mystery.

Another foe of Indra in the age of the mantras was Krishṇa, a god or deified hero of a tribe called the Krishṇas. Of him it is said, "The fleet Krishṇa lived on the banks of the Ams'umatī (Jumna) river with ten thousand troops. Indra of his own wisdom became cognizant of this loud-yelling chief. He destroyed the marauding host for the benefit of (Ārya) men. Indra said, 'I have seen the fleet Krishṇa. He is lurking in the hidden region near the Ams'umatī, like the sun in a cloud. O Maruts, I desire you to engage him in fight and to destroy him. The fleet Krishṇa then appeared shining on the banks of the Ams'umatī. Indra took Brihaspati as his ally and destroyed the fleet and godless army." (R. V. viii. 85. 13—15). Indra with Rijis'vā, son of Vidathī, killed the pregnant wives of Krishna (*Ib.* i. 101. 1, ii. 20—7). Indra smote 50,000 Krishṇas, as old age destroys the body (R. V. iv. 16—13). European scholars have interpreted d r a p s a ḥ K r i s h ṇ a ḥ in the first of these passages as the 'black drop,' possibly because they believe that the Krishṇa-cult rose later; but there is absolutely no reason why beliefs on *a priori* grounds should over-ride Indian tradition which makes Krishṇa one of Indra's seven demon-foes, he "who never had met a rival" till Indra was born (R. V. viii. 85. 16). In fact the translation "black drop" makes the whole passage meaningless. Krishṇa was the enemy of Indra throughout the whole course of the development of religion in India. The Purāṇas, which certainly contain very old legends, many as old as the Vedic age, describe many conflicts between Indra and Krishṇa, in one of which, Krishṇa put an end to the worship of Indra on the banks of this very Jumna, among the tribes that lived in the woods near the river. The phrase '*fleet* Krishna' vividly brings home to us that he was from early days the god of wandering pastoral tribes; probably called the Vrishṇis—the *ram* tribe. The antagonism of the Krishna-cult to the Indra-cult not only recurs constantly in the legends but a far-off echo of it is heard even in the B h a g a v a d-G ī t a where Krishna refers scornfully to the "flowery words" of the "fools," who delight in the Vedas, which as we know were born from the Indra cult, and which Krishṇa advises his followers to reject because they bewilder the mind (ii. 42, 45, 46, 53). And Krishṇa, the god of the early Indian pastoral tribes, became the nucleus round which gathered other tales, possibly of human heroes, other cults, *e g.*, the Vāsudeva-cult of the

Bhāgavatas, the Vishṇu-cult of the Vaishṇavas till to-day, Krishṇa-worship is the dominating religion of India and the Indra-cult practically dead. It is also interesting to note that notwithstanding the accretion of so many tales round the name of Krishṇa, it is the cowherd playing the flute to his cattle on the banks of the Jumna and sporting with the simple village maidens that still appeals to the mind of the Hindu.

The higher thinkers of the Vedic age had developed a strong sense of cosmic law and of moral law. The cosmic order was called r i t a m or v r a t a m and was under the guardianship of the higher gods. The same words designated moral order, truth in the moral world and rite in the religious world (R. V. i. 84. 4, viii. 25. 2). Vishnu, the unconquerable preserver, strode three steps and thereby established fixed laws (R. V. i. 22. 18). The order of Varuṇa and Mitra is established where the steeds of the sun are loosed. (R. V. v. 62-1). By Varuṇa's ordinances the moon shines brightly through night and the stars on high are seen at night and disappear by day (R. V. i. 24.10). Varuṇa rules over these worlds and beholds everything as if he were close at hand. He knows all things, even deeds done by stealth (A. V. iv. 16-1). He casts his noose on the man who speaks lies (A. V. iv. 16-6). By Savitā's commands, "the wild beasts spread through desert places seeking their watery share which thou hast set in waters. The woods are given to the birds. These statutes of the god Savitā none disobeyeth. With utmost speed, in restless haste at sunset, Varuṇa seeks his watery habitation. Then seeks each bird his nest, each beast his lodging. In due place Savitā hath set each creature" (R. V. ii. 38. 7. 8). Indra established the lights of the sky (R. V. viii. 14-9). By his skill he has propped up the sky from falling (R. V. ii.

17-5). "The sun and the moon move alternately, O Indra, that we may behold and have faith" (R. V. i. 102-2). Agni formed the regions of the earth and the luminaries of heaven (R. V. vi. 7. 7) and his ordinances cannot be resisted (R. V. ii. 8. 3). He is the guardian of immortality (R. V. vii. 7. 7) and forgives sins committed through folly (R. V. iv. 12. 4). The thread of R i t a m, wherein the gods, obtaining life eternal, have risen upward to one common birth place, extends far." (A. V. ii. 1. 5).

The creation of the earth, of men and of gods was conceived in various ways. It was built by Vis'vakarmā, as a carpenter fashions a house or a car out of wood. (R. V. x. 31. 7). It was produced by Brahmaṇaspati with blast and smelting as a blacksmith forges things of metal. (R. V. x. 72. 2). Heaven and earth generated the gods as men do children. "Prolific (s u r e t a s ā) parents, they have made the world of life" (R. V. i. 159. 2). Another primeval pair were Daksha and Aditi and after them were born the gods, who formed the worlds by agitating the waters (R. V. x. 72. 5—6). The gods themselves came from a germ in the waters. "That which is beyond the sky, beyond this earth, beyond the devas and the asuras—what earliest germ did the waters contain, in which all the gods were beheld? The waters contained that earliest embryo in which all the gods were collected. The one rested upon the naval of the unborn, wherein all beings stood." Creation, again, was due to the sacrifice of the primeval being, p u r u s h a. The devas "bound the p u r u s h a as a (sacrificial) animal, spring was the ghi, summer was the fuel and autumn the (accompanying) oblation. They cut him down, placed him on the sacred grass, the devas, Sādhyas and Rishis divided his body and from it were produced all creatures (R. V. x. 90). The world was also conceived to be evolved from the one, which previous to creation, when all was enveloped in darkness, breathed without air. Desire (k ā m a) first arose in it; this was the first germ of mind. The gods, themselves, arose afterwards (R. V. x. 129).

Even in this early age the minds of some men in ancient India rose above the interests of war, the acquisition of wealth and happiness by sacrifice or by spells, by war or by trade and above the carnal enjoyments of this world or the next. Their keen vision pierced through the phenomena of the world to what is beyond. Dīrghatamas, son of Mamatā, propounded the question, "I ask, unknowing, those who know, the sages, as one all ignorant for the sake of knowledge, what was that one, who in the unborn's image hath established and fixed firm these six regions of the world" (R. V. i. 164. 6). Gotama saw Aditi in the heaven, Aditi in mid-air, Aditi in all the gods, in the five races of men, Aditi in all that has been born and in all that shall be born (R. V. i. 89. 10). Vis'vāmitra asked "what pathway leadeth to the gods? Who knoweth this of a truth, and who will now declare it? Seen are their lowest dwellings (heavenly bodies) only; but they are in remote and secret regions" (iii. 54. 5) and saw behind the many gods the One "Lord of what is fixed and moving, that walks, that flies, this multiform creation" (*Ib.* 8). Another seer saw one being throughout the world, Skambha, to whom all paths tended, into whom all entered. To him all the gods are joined as branches around the trunk of a tree. He abides in the human body that is the nine-portalled lotus flower and "desireless, firm, immortal, self-existent, contented with the essence, lacking nothing, free from fear of death is he who knoweth that soul (ā t m ā) courageous, youthful, undecaying" (A. V. x. 8. 44).

This tendency to the higher monotheism, as distinguished from the tribal monotheism of savages led to the definite distribution of functions among the gods. Thus Agni became the overlord of the East and the Adityas his arrows, Indra of the South, the fathers his arrows, Varuṇa of the West, Soma of the North, Vishṇu of the fixed quarter and Brihaspati of the upward quarter (A. V. v. 27). This also led to the famous triple classification of the gods, which though begun into the age of the Mantras, yet dominates the interpretation of Vedic mythology; for even in early times the gods were divided into those of earth and of heaven and dwellers in the waters (R. V. vi. 50. 11, vii. 35. 11, i. 139. 11, x. 49. 2, x. 65. 9). A. V. x. 9. 12 divides them into the gods that are stationed in the sky, and that are stationed in the atmosphere and these that are upon the earth," thus indicating that the "waters" of the passages of the Rig Veda quoted above was the atmospheric ocean. This is the beginning of the division of the gods that the Nirukta of a later age popularized and modern scholars have accepted almost without criticism.

Omniscience as a divine characteristic was attributed by the Rishis to Varuṇa. "The great guardian among these (gods) sees as if from a near. He that thinketh he is moving stealthily, all this the gods know. If a man stands, walks, or sneaks about, if he goes slinking away, if he goes into his hiding place; if two persons sit together and scheme, King Varuṇa is there as a third and knows it. Both this earth here belongs to King Varuṇa, and also yonder broad sky whose boundaries are far away. Moreover these two oceans are the loins of Varuṇa: yea, he is hidden in this small drop of water. He that should flee beyond the heaven far away would not be free from King Varuṇa. His spies come hither (to the earth) from heaven, with a thousand eyes do they watch over the earth King Varuṇa sees through all that it between heaven and earth, and all that it beyond He has counted the winkings of men's eyes. As a (winning) gamester puts down his dice, thus does he establish these (laws)." (A. V. iv. 16. 1—5). Notwithstanding this remarkable statement of divine Omniscience it was not Varuṇa that led to the conception of the One Deity so much as Vis'vakarmā, Prajāpati and above all Brahma. Vis'vakarmā was "the one god who has eyes on every side, on every side a face, arms every side, feet every side, who, when producing the sky and earth, shapes them with his arms and with his bellows" (R. V. x. 81. 3). "He who is our father, our creator, disposer, who knows all spheres and creatures, who alone assigns to gods their names, to him the other creatures resort for instruction" (R. V. x. 82. 3). Of Prajāpati, it is said, "Prajāpati moves in the womb. Being unborn, he is born in many shapes. The wise behold his womb. In him all the worlds stand" (S. Y. S. xxxi. 19). "He before whom nothing was born, who pervades all worlds is Prajāpati, who rejoices with his offspring" (S. Y. S. xxxii. 5). But when the concept of the One Being was clearly evolved, Brahma was the name given to it. Brahma is "the greatest, who presides over the past, the future, the Universe, and whose alone is the sky" (A. V. x. 8 1). In the S. Y. S. xxiii 47 is put the question "What light is equal to the sun? What lake is equal to the sea?" The next verse supplies the answer, "Brahma is the light equal to the sun; the sky is the lake equal to the sea." This is the root of the Vedānta conception of the root of being expounded in innumerable ways in the Brāhmaṇams generally and more especially in their latest chapters called the Upanishads. The worship of Brahma by means of meditation was the aim of ascetic orders who gave up the sacrifices to Indra and the other gods. Bādarayaṇa in a later age attempted to give unity to the various expositions of the concept, Brahma, by laying down the rules of exegesis included in his Brahma Mīmāmsa Sūtras. Pāṇini calls them Bhikshu Sūtras (iv. 3. 110), as they were intended for ascetics. But these, again, have been, in the last thousand years, pressed into service to serve as the foundations of the dogmas of S'ankara, Rāmanuja, Ānandatīrtha and many other modern theologians who themselves founded ascetic orders but whose pessimistic teachings have later been thrown open to the man in the street and have helped to rob him of his joy of life.

This sketch of the life of the people of Ancient India in the second millennium B.C. proves how little India has changed these four thousand years. Almost every custom, every institution referred to in this book can be yet observed, every mantra translated can be heard, every image described can be seen in thousands of villages to-day, even those wherefrom one can hear the panting of the steam-engine and the hoot of the motor-horn. And this, notwithstanding that during this long period India has witnessed numerous volcanic upheavals of society like that which was caused by the spread of the teachings of the Jina and the Buddha, notwithstanding the tremendous thunderstorms that have broken over India from the invasion of Alexander of Macedon down to the invasion of Baber the Mogul. The conservative instincts of man, his averseness to change of all kinds, which dominated Europe up to the Age of the French Revolution still hold India in their icy grip and affords us this spectacle of a people that have remained unchangeable as their own Himālaya during the shocks of ages.

INDEX.